ANCIENT AND MEDIEVAL NEPAL

Ancient and Medieval Nepal

RISHIKESH SHAHA

MANOHAR
2026

First published 1992
Reprinted 2026

ISBN 978-81-7304-402-1

Published by
Ajay Kumar Jain *for*
Manohar Publishers & Distributors
4753/23 Ansari Road, Daryaganj
New Delhi 110 002

Printed and bound in India

CONTENTS

FOREWORD

As the year 1991 dawns Nepal is on the threshold of a new era. A new constitution vests sovereignity in the people, and the first multi-party elections for a House of Representatives under the new constitution have just been concluded. A fresh wind is blowing across the land, and all eyes are on the vision of a new and bright future. One might ask: What is the relevance at this point in time of a new book on Ancient and Medieval Nepal?

An answer to that question is given by a character in one of Nayantara Sahgal's novels:

> There are governments called people's governments that are really built on the destruction of a people's whole foundation. Not only have they overthrown a tyranny but a religion and a philosophy as well, and tossed away an accumulation of racial experience. Revolutions, have to take place when living conditions become intolerable, but even a revolution should not destroy a people's framework. It should stop short of that. Tear that down and you will have a bewildered society, people who've lost their moorings and don't know where they're going.[1]

It is precisely at this juncture that a nation must ask itself: Who are we? Where have we come from?, and Where are we going? No viable answer can be given to the third question without some reflection on the first two. Failure to root the new order in the culture and tradition of the nation will produce a "bewildered society, people who've lost their moorings and don't know where they're going".

Mr. Rishikesh Shaha is well qualified to undertake such a study. On one side his family roots strech back to the princely state of Bhirkot in the hills of Nepal. The culture and tradition of Nepal is an amalgam of the traditions of these small hill kingdoms and the kingdoms of the Valley. On the other side his family roots reach into the family of Bir Shamsher, one of the longest ruling of the Rana Prime Ministers. Yet Mr. Shaha has been actively involved in all the modern political movements and experiments of Nepal from the days, when as a young lecturer in Tri-Chandra College, he read the English newspapers to Padma Shamsher, the Rana Prime Minister who took the first timorous steps towards Democracy.

He was actively involved in the political movements which resulted from the overthrow of the Ranas. During the time of the first elected government he served as Nepal's permanent representative to the United Nations and later served as Nepal's Foreign Minister. The first draft of the present book was the fruit of a period of enforced leisure when he was removed from public office and arrested. Since that time he has written and lectured widely on politics in modern Nepal, always the gadfly who nurtured the flame of democratic ideals and concern for human rights.

The first draft of this work was written over twenty years ago. The intervening years have seen a wealth of research on Ancient and Medieval Nepal, mostly by Nepali scholars. Over the past two years Mr. Shaha has revised the original to include the latest scholarship. There are other books in English on these two periods, notably the pioneering works of Dr. Dilli Raman Regmi. However, few ordinary readers will take the time to work through five volumes.

It has been a privilege to be associated with Mr. Shaha in the revision of this work and its preparation for the press. I can only hope that the present volume will be of use to those who must now shape the destiny of this nation and to the many foreign friends of Nepal. Many of these friends are occasional visitors to Nepal, attracted to the stunning beauty of the country and the friendliness of her people. They long to know more about them. Others come to assist in the process of development, an impossible task without some knowledge of who these people are and where they came from.

John K. Locke, S.J.

1. Nayantara Sahgal, *Storm in Chandigarh*. Delhi, Orient Paperbacks, n.d. p. 11.

PREFACE

I wrote the first draft of *Ancient and Medieval Nepal* during solitary confinement in jail in the years 1969-70. As I had plenty of time at my disposal, I not only read all the available books on the subject in Nepali and English but also took the opportunity to put the substance of what I had read into a coherent and readable narrative. It was my friend, Meg Sheffield, who was the first reader and who helped me greatly by carefully reading every word in the text.

However, the draft then lay idle, catching dust in my study, for nearly twenty years. During this interval, a good deal of work on the subject was done by Nepali and foreign scholars, and there was no point in publishing my book without doing justice to their contributions.

It was Dr. John Locke S.J. who helped me in updating the manuscript by incorporating the latest research on the subject. Had it not been for his generous and substantial assistance, the book would never have seen print. Let me take this opportunity to record my profound gratitude and indebtedness to him, and my acknowledgments to the journal *Kailash* in which the book was serialised.

Rishikesh Shaha

16 June 1991
Kathmandu

LIST OF ILLUSTRATIONS

CHAPTER I

INTRODUCTION

Geographical Setting

The kingdom of Nepal, an elongated rectangle lying along the slopes of the mighty Himalaya, stretches for five hundred miles from east to west and lies between 80° and 88° East Longitude. Barely a hundred miles wide and stretching from 26° to 30° North Latitude, its altitudes range from a few feet above sea level to the highest point on earth. The variety of elevations gives the country a range of climatic zones encompassing almost all those found on earth, from the subtropical jungle to the arctic conditions of the high Himalaya and the arid zone of the Tibetan plateau. With an area of 54,717 square miles and a population of 17,000,000 Nepal is hardly a tiny country--70% of the member nations of the United Nations are smaller than Nepal in terms of population and over 40% are smaller in terms of area. Yet she is dwarfed by her two giant neighbours, India and China.

If one approaches the country from the south the first hills encountered are the Chure Hills rising sharply from the Gangetic plain to an average of 3,000 feet.[1] This band of hills, five to ten miles wide, presents a rugged, forested landscape with dry and immature soils. North of this range rises the Mahabharat Lekh or 'mid-hills' to an average of 7,000 ft. above sea level, though individual peaks may be as high as 9,000 ft. The hills are steep and jagged with the lower slopes cleared and terraced for cultivation and the upper slopes covered with forest. Fifty miles north of the Mahabharat Lekh rise the mighty Himalaya. Nepal has over 240 peaks above 20,000 ft. above sea level and the queen of these is Sagarmatha (Mount Everest). This is a wild and rugged landscape with a permanent snow line above 17,000 ft. and few human inhabitants.

The ranges of hills alternate with lowland areas. Along the Indian border is the Tarai or 'Madesh' area, a continuation of the Gangetic plain. This 25-35 mile wide belt is a land of subtropical forest and farms. Between the Chure and Mahabharat ranges are narrow, low valleys known as 'Dun' which resemble the 'Tarai' in climate and relief. Between the Mahabharat range and the Himalaya lies the 'Hill Country' or 'Pahāṛ Country' which includes the narrow, north-south valleys of the great rivers: the Karnali, the Gandaki and the Kosi. Since the high Himalaya is uninhabitable and until recent times most of the Tarai was a malaria-infested jungle, this 'Hill Country' has been the traditional area of Nepali settlement. Here lies the Valley of Kathmandu, the capital and nerve centre of Modern Nepal and the cradle of Nepali culture.

West of the meridian of the Kathmandu Valley and north of the main range of the Himalaya lies yet another range known as the Tibetan marginal mountains extending north for about twenty miles. These mountains average 19,000 ft. above sea level and the terrain is less rugged than that of the Himalaya. Between the high Himalaya and these mountains lie a number of high valleys called 'Bhot' valleys with a landscape similar to that of Tibet.

Geography has determined the very existence of Nepal as a separate nation. It has determined her culture, and her economy. Each of the lowland areas of the country the Tarai, the Hill Country, and the Bhot Valleys has its own distinctive environment, population and economy. Over the centuries this hill area has provided a haven for people from north and south, so that the present racial make-up of the country is a mixture of various Asian elements which has been called the 'ethnic turntable of Asia'.

King Pṛithvinārāyaṇa Śāha of Gorkha united the petty kingdoms across the hills into one nation in the latter part of the seventeenth century, but the kingdom of Nepal has a long history and the extent of the country has varied according to the fortunes of the various dynasties.

Sources

Though we have contemporary written records from the fifth century A.D. on, the origins of Nepal are still shrouded in a veil of mystery. Nepal is mentioned in several of the classical Indian sources and we have several classical literary sources of Nepali origin such as the *Purāṇas* the *Paśupati Purāṇa*, the *Himavat Khaṇḍa*, the *Nepāla Mahātmya*, and the *Svayambhu Purāṇa*. Yet these are fairly late works and not works of history but mythologies rich in religious and cultural lore.

A number of vaṃśāvalīs or chronicles give us some information about the origins and earliest history of Nepal. The oldest and most reliable of these is called the *Gopālarājavaṃśāvalīs* ('The Chronicle of the Gopāla Kings'). The first half of this chronicle is written in Sanskrit of a rather corrupt and ungrammatical quality; the second half is in medieval Newari with a preponderance of Indo-Aryan loan words.[2] It is written in one of the earliest scripts used in Nepal known as *bhuji mola* or 'the fly-headed script' which apparently resembles the Gupta or Kutila script and which, according to Prof. Kamal P. Malla, is the palaeographic successor of the ancient Newari script with hooked lines. Internal evidence and the special praise bestowed upon King Sthitirāja Malla (A.D. 1382-95) as Rāma, Buddha and Lokapāla reveals that the final redaction of this chronicle belongs to the last quarter of the fourteenth century though the Sanskrit section may be older.

The chronicle which William J. Kirkpatrick drew on when compiling his list of rulers and the length of their reigns seems to be equally old and reliable. The chronicle from the private collection of the late Field Marshal Kaiser Shamsher Jang Bahadur Rana, which was used by Luciano Petech in his book *Medieval History of Nepal*, seems to be an abridged version of the chronicle used by Kirkpatrick in his work, *An Account of The Kingdom of Nepal* (1811).[3]

The later chronicles all written in the Nepali language in the last century are merely new versions of the aforementioned Sanskrit and classical Newari works with subsequent additions, condensations and adaptations. Some of the Nepali language chronicles which have acquired a good deal of prominence, as a result of their use by foreign authors in their works on Nepal, are those contained in (1) *History of Nepal Translated from the Parbatiya* (1877) by Dr. Daniel Wright,[4] (ii) 'Some Considerations on the History of Nepal', by Bhagvanlal Indraji and Buhler[5], (iii) *Le Nepal*, étude historique d'un Royaume Hindou, by Sylvain Levi,[6] and 'A History of Nepal and Surrounding Kingdoms (1000- 1600)', by Cecil Bendall[7], later reprinted as the introduction to H. P. Shastri's *Catalogue of Palmleaf and Selected Paper Manuscripts Belonging to the Darbar Library, Nepal.*[8]. Three more of these chronicles have been published in more recent times in Nepali and several more lie unpublished in the National Archives. All four of the chronicles used by the authors mentioned above seem to be more or less identical, although they were compiled for them by different local persons at different times. The chronicle used by Wright was initially translated for him into English by Munshi Shewasankar of the British Residency with the help of a local Nepali, Gubhaju Gunananda. The chronicles used by Sylvain Levi were compiled for him by Siddhi Narayan of Deupatan, Kathmandu. A Nepali gentleman named Kharidar Buddhiman Singh compiled, translated, and edited such chronicles in Nepali up till the 1870s. All the subsequent Nepali language chronicles may derive from the version compiled by him and completed in 1878.

Though the chronicles are not primarily historical works in the modern sense, the dynastic framework or chronology which they furnish for the later periods has been corroborated by epigraphic and numismatic evidence. For the earliest period of Nepal's history, they provide an imposing list of dynastic rulers, constructed by compilers writing at a much later date. Often historians have omitted some of the names of the rulers given in the chronicles because they are found to be either too many or too few to cover the period.

Grateful mention must also be made of basic works on Nepali and Indian numismatics and epigraphy by E. H. Walsh, A. Cunningham, J. F. Fleet and F. Kielhorn who have provided material useful to the study of the ancient and medieval history of Nepal.

Archeological investigations carried out in several parts of the country have also added to our knowledge of the ancient period. Excavations at Tilaurakot, Beniarahi and Paisia in the Nepal Tarai have furnished evidence of the existence of civilization in that area before 300 B.C. Although the cultural influence of the Maurya and Sung empires during the three centuries before Christ had definitely made its way into the Nepal Tarai, limited excavations at Hadigaun, Lajimpat and Dhum Varahi in Kathmandu have not so far yielded proof of settlements in the Valley prior to the early centuries of the Christian era.

The chronicles are the only source covering the earliest period of Nepali history for which no epigraphic or numismatic evidence is available. It is only after the middle of the fifth century A.D. that inscriptions enter the picture. From the 10th century onward an invaluable source of authentic historical information is found in the colophons of manuscripts of various literary works. A colophon is a note placed at the end of a manuscript usually giving the name of the scribe, the date, the place the manuscript was copied, the name of the reigning monarch, and frequently one or two other bits of information. Thanks to the arduous labours of Daniel Wright, Bhagvanlal Indraji, Harapada Das Chattopadhyaya, Cecil Bendall, Sylvain Levi and K. P. Jayaswal in the past and of Raniero Gnoli, Luciano Petech and Giuseppi Tucci, in our time, inscriptions and colophons from different periods and from different parts of Nepal were collected, published and interpreted. Over the last twenty-five years more of these have been collected, published and interpreted by Nepali scholars especially by a group of Nepali scholars known as the *Itihās Saṃsodhan Maṇḍal* under the direction of Naya Raj Pant. Dhanavajra Vajracarya, one of the scholars of this group, has published the entire corpus of the early inscriptions with a Nepali translation and commentary[9] and Dr. Dilli Raman Regmi has recently published them again with an English translation and commentary.[10] The individual labour of an ascetic of the Gorakhanath sect, Yogi Narharinath, has resulted in the collection of a fair number of inscriptions and other source materials from various parts of the country.

These works have furnished a valuable fund of epigraphical information and made it possible for scholars to assess the substance and detail of the chronicle information in the light of more positive and authentic historical evidence. Strange as it may seem to modern historians, the writing of the early history of Nepal has so far been mainly an attempt to order the chronological list of dynastic rulers, and even at that, as Prof. Petech suggests, with a touch of irony and humour, 'the list is by no means a settled one.'[11]

Another source available to us from the eleventh century, is on what is known as *tāḍ patra tamasuks*. These are legal documents (*tamasuk*) recording land grants, land transactions, loans and other monetary transactions written on narrow strips of palm leaf (*tāḍ patra*). These provide a wealth of information on the political, economic and social status of the country.[12] From the late Malla period we also have a number of *thyāsaphus*, personal diaries of events mainly pertaining to the life of the royal courts.[13]

Early Works

The first article published in English on Nepal was Sir John Shore's translation of Father Giuseppe de Rovato's 'An Account of the Kingdom of Nepal,' in the second volume of the *Asiatic Researches* (Calcutta), in 1790. Fr. Giuseppe's account, however, belongs to an earlier period, as he died in 1786. Col. William Kirkpatrick's *An Account of the Kingdom of Nepal*, containing information gathered during his 1793 diplomatic mission to Kathmandu is the first complete book on Nepal in English and was brought out by Miller, London in 1811. Another very early book on Nepal was *An Account of the Kingdom of Nepal and of the Territories Annexed to this Dominion by the House of Gorkha*, by Dr. Francis Buchanan (later Hamilton), published in 1819 by Constable, Edinburgh.

Among the Nepali authors in the field, Ambika Prasad Upadhyaya was the first to write and publish a history of Nepal in Nepali (1929). His book is, however, based entirely on secondary information derived by the author from his perusal of books in English. Following in his footsteps Totra Raj Pande, Balachandra Sharma and Dhundiraj Bhandari wrote and published books in Nepali on the history of Nepal. Baburam Acharya, Surya Bikram Gewali and Nayaraj Pant deserve mention among the more serious Nepali scholars of the country's history, and it is mainly to them that the Nepali reading public owes its knowledge of the country's past. Dr. Jagadish Regmi has made a remarkable contribution to the history of ancient Nepal with his three books in Nepali on Licchavi Culture, the political history of the period and the religious history of the period. Dr. Dilli Raman Regmi is the only Nepali historian who has written and published extensively in English on the ancient and medieval history of the country. His *Ancient Nepal* and his three-volume *Inscriptions of Ancient Nepal* deal with the earliest period. His four volumes on Medieval Nepal, comprising 2,249 pages, are a monumental collection of source materials for a study of the period.

Nepal in Legend and Myth

The *vaṃśāvalīs* or chronicles take us back to the very origins of the country and tell us how the Kathmandu Valley, which was once a lake, was rendered fit for human habitation by Krishna or *Mañjuśrī*, either of whom may be credited with the feat of cutting a deep gorge in the mountain to drain the water. Geological evidence confirms that the Valley was indeed a lake at one time. Its rich, moist soil must have produced a luxuriant growth of vegetation. The newly reclaimed land and its virgin forests must have provided an ideal habitat and ample food for both the domesticated cattle and the wild life that abounded in the area during the time of the first settlers.

The chronicles are literary rather than historical compositions. However, if one takes as generic names the names they give for the earliest ruling dynasties, namely the Gopālas (cowherds) and the Mahiṣapālas (the buffalo-herders), then the imaginative accounts of their adventures prove realistic enough as general descriptions of the pastoral stage of civilization prior to the practice of settled agricultural life.

As a manifestation of divine will or as a mere dispensation of nature, a sage (*muni*) called Ne appears on the scene as the protector (*pāla*) of the land and the founder of the first ruling dynasty. Thus the chronicles explain the origin of the name of the country Ne-pāla, the land 'protected by Ne'. His successors are called *gopālavaṃśi*, the members or descendants of the family of cowherds. Curiously enough, their names end in —*gupta*; and this makes sense, in a way, because the well-known latter day Gupta rulers of India and Nepal (A.D. 320-550) also claimed descent from the cowherds. According to the chronicle used by Kirkpatrick, the *gopālavaṃśi*, or the cowherd family, some with names ending in '—*gupta*', cover a period of four hundred and ninety-one years.

It was customary for the Nepali and Indian rulers to trace their lineage to some worthy personage, human or divine. As the sun and the moon are generally regarded as gods, and were visible to everyone, the rulers felt a natural temptation to claim descent from them. The Cowherd (*gopāla*) Dynasty, claiming descent from the moon is called either the Lunar (*candravaṃśi*) or the Ne Muni Dynasty. The chronicles used by Kirkpatrick and Wright name eight kings of this dynasty, whereas Padmagiri's chronicle mentions only five.[14]

According to Kirkpatrick's chronicle, the Cowherd Dynasty is followed by rulers of the Buffalo-herder Dynasty (*mahiṣapālavaṃśa*), founded by an Indian Rajput called Bhul Singh. He came from the country between Simraungarh and Janakpur in the Nepal Tarai. He and his two successors, Jaya Singh and Bhavāni Singh, are said to have ruled for a total of eleven years and seven months. Other chronicles mention three kings of this short-lived dynasty which they call the 'Abhira' ('Ahir') Dynasty: Varasiṃha, Jayamatisiṃha and Bhuvansiṃha.

The village of Matatirtha, situated at a distance of four miles southwest of Kathmandu, was the seat of government of the rulers of the Cowherd and Buffalo-herder dynasties. Nepal was then bounded by the River Trisuli on the west, by the River Dudhkosi on the east, by the Nilakantha Himalayan range on the north, and by the valley of Chitlang on the south.

The last ruler of the Buffalo-herder Dynasty was overthrown by the Kirāta army of Yellung Kirāta, from the region beyond the River Dudhkosi which extended as far as the kingdom of the Devarāja of Bhutan to the east. According to Kirkpatrick's chronicle, Yellung Kirāta was succeeded by twenty-six rulers of the Kirāta Dynasty whose rule covered a total period of one thousand five hundred and eighty-one years and one month.[15] Quite a few rulers thus must have reigned more than fifty years and some for more than seventy years, or the lengths of these reigns have been arbitrarily doubled or trebled to fill up the time span. The names of the kings do not sound Sanskritic. The list begins with Yellung, Duskham, Ballancha, etc. and ends with Khembhoom and Gully Jung, the latter being assigned the incredibly long reign of eighty-one years.[16]

Although these rulers have been given inconceivably long reigns in the above account, it is with the Kirātas that the chronicles reach slightly more solid ground above the boggy realm of myth and legend. The Kirātas have a good deal more than the shadowy existence of their predecessors in the chronicle accounts, for they still exist. The Rais and Limbus of eastern Nepal are collectively known as Kirātīs to this day. The Kirātas are also celebrated in the well-known Hindu epic, the *Mahābhārata* and in the *Purāṇas* as a hill-tribe with remarkable skill in archery and warfare. Although there is no direct or precise reference to Kirāta rule in the inscriptions of the later rulers, there can be little doubt that the Kirātas ruled for a few centuries before Licchavi rule began in Nepal. Numerous place names are recorded in the Licchavi inscriptions which are non-Sanskrit and are taken to be of Kirāta origin.

Nothing substantial is known about Nepal's relations with either the Nanda empire (4th Century B. C.) or the Maurya empire (c. 325-185 B.C.) except for stray references in Buddhist and Jaina religious literature, to the account of Aśoka's visit to Lumbini (the birthplace of the Buddha), and the popular legend of his visit to the Kathmandu Valley. Hence we do not know for certain whether Nepal came under the sway of the Nanda and the Maurya rulers. Nor is it certain whether or not Nepal came under Kuśāna rule which extended from about the middle of the first century A.D. to the third century. Some historians have claimed that Nepal did come under the Kuśāna rulers but solely on the basis of the discovery in the Valley of stray coins of the Kuśāna emperors, Kadiphes I and II.[17] It may be surmised that the supremacy of the Kirātas and their Licchavi successors did correspond to the later period of Kuśāna rule, but the present state of our knowledge does not allow us to state anything definite about the extent of Kuśāna domination over the Kathmandu Valley.

When the Licchavis, who succeeded the Kirātas, entered Nepal and when they assumed their position of power is not known. According to one theory, the Licchavis entered Nepal about the middle of the 5th century B.C., after Vaisali was overrun around 464 B.C. by Ajātaśatru, king of Magadha and the first ruthless empire builder. On the other hand, the Licchavis may have entered Nepal only after the Licchavi homeland of Vaisali fell under the control of the Kuśānas, in which case they would not have set up their dynasty in Nepal until the

1st or 2nd century of the Christian era. It seems that there was indeed a wave of migration of peoples from northern Bihar to the Nepal hills. This is suggested by the existence of the Koliyas, Vrjikas and Śākyas in the Kathmandu Valley. Most probably the Mallas first migrated to the Gandaki basin.

With the exception of the *Gopālarājavaṃśāvalī*, the chronicles do not mention the Licchavis by name but merely proceed with a new list of kings. Except for the one used by Kirkpatrick, all the chronicles list some of the rulers who followed the Kirāta kings as belonging to the Lunar Dynasty (*somavaṃśī*) and some to the Solar Dynasty (*sūryavaṃśī*). According to Kirkpatrick's chronicle, the Kirātas were dispossessed of their kingdom by Nevesit, a Kśhatriya of the Solar Dynasty, who set up his own dynastic rule. The fact that the *Gopālarājavaṃśāvalīs* has been definitive about the rise of the Licchavis to power following the downfall of the Kirātas proves the importance of this work. The *Paśupati Purāṇa* is also of the same view. The Licchavis themselves claimed descent from the sun-god as Jayadeva II has recorded in his Pashupati inscription of A.D. 733. These Lunar and Solar Dynasties also link the Nepali rulers, like most of the north Indian dynasties, to the great epic heroes of the *Rāmāyaṇa* and the *Mahābhārata*, who also claimed similar origins from the moon and sun gods of the Hindu myths.

NOTES

1. Based on Harka Bahadur. Gurung, 'Geographic Setting', in *Nepal, A Profile*, Kathmandu, Nepal Council of Applied Economic Research, 1970, p. 4-11. The terminology is his.
2. Dhanavajra Vajracarya and Kamal P. Malla eds., tr. *The Gopālarājavaṃśavalī*. Nepal Research Centre Publications No. 9. Wiesbaden Franz Steiner Verlag, 1985.
3. Colonel Kirkpatrick, *An Account of the Kingdom of Nepaul* (1811), New Delhi, Manjusri Publishing House, 1969.
4. Reprint: Kathmandu, Nepal Antiquated Book Publishers, 1972.
5. Bhagvanlal Indraji, "Twenty-three Inscriptions from Nepal with some Considerations on the Chronology of Nepal", translated from Gujarati by G. Buhler. Reprinted from *Indian Antiquary* Vol IX (1880) 163-94.
6. Paris, Ernest Leroux, 1908.
7. *Journal of the Asiatic Society of Bengal*, 72 (1903) 1-32.
8. Calcutta, Baptist Mission Press, 1916.
9. Dhanavajra, Vajracarya, *Licchavīkālkā Abhilekh*, Kathmandu, Institute of Nepal and Asian Studies, Historical Collections Series, no. 6., 1973.
10. Dilli Raman Regmi, *Inscriptions of Ancient Nepal*, 3 Vols. New Delhi, Abhinav Publications, 1983.

11. Luciano Petech,. *Medieval History of Nepal*, Roma: Instituto Italiano per il Medio ed Estremo Oriente, 1958, p. 5.
12. A number of these have been published in various Nepali journals. Shankarman Rajvamsi has published three volumes of them under the title *Bhūmiśaṃsbandhī Tamasuk Tāḍpatra*. Hemraj Sakya has published the oldest collection of these found at Uku Baha in Patan (*Śivadeva Saṃskārita Uṅkulī Śrī Rudravarṇa Mahāvihāra Sthita Tālpatra-Abhilekh* [Patan: Buddha Jayanti Samiti, 2524 Buddha Samvat]). Sixty Eight of these have been published with English translation and commentary by Barnhard Kolver and Hemraj Sakya (*Documents from the Rudravarṇa Mahāvihāra, Patan*. Sankt Augustin, VGH-Wissenschaftsverlag, 1985).
13. A *thysāphu* is a manuscript written on a continuous strip of heavy card-board-like Nepali paper which is compressed into different folds so that it opens like an accordian.
14. Kirkpatrick p. 256; Wright, Daniel ed. *History of Nepal*, Calcutta, Ranjan Gupta, 1977.
15. Kirkpatrick pp. 257-8.
16. *Ibid.*
17. D.R. Regmi, *Ancient Nepal*, Calcutta, Firma K.L. Mukhopadhyay, 1960, pp. 69-73.

CHAPTER II

THE LICCHAVI ERA

(5th Century A.D. to Mid 9th Century)

Though it is not known exactly when the Licchavis penetrated into Nepal, there is a consensus among historians that the Licchavi rule in Nepal must have commenced by the first or the second century of the Christian era. However, the names of some seventeen or eighteen rulers that follow Nevesit in the chronicle confront us with a problem. The question is whether to accept these rulers as Licchavi rulers, even in the absence of epigraphical and numismatic evidence about them, or to treat at least the first five (Nevesit, Makaranta, Kakavarman, Paśupuṣpa Deva and Bhāskara Varman) as belonging to the Lunar Dynasty (*somavaṃśī*) and the rest to the Solar Dynasty (*sūryavaṃśī*), as most of the chronicles do.[1] The chronicle to which Kirkpatrick owes his information has made the problem a little simpler by accepting all the rulers as members of the Solar Dynasty, to which the Licchavis themselves belonged. Even then, the problem of accounting for the lengthy reigns of these seventeen or eighteen rulers persists.

Dr. D. R. Regmi has ascribed to Paśupuṣpa Deva the revival of Hindu influence in the Kathmandu Valley, which had been dominated for some time by Mahāyāna Buddhism under the patronage of the Kuśānas.[2] He regards Bhāskara Varman, whom the chronicles (obviously in a spirit of exaggeration) credit with the conquest of India up to Rameshvaram in the south, as the solar splendour of the Licchavis in fact as well as in name. He further infers from the above that the support of the Licchavis in Nepal was solidly entrenched behind the Guptas in India. The mention of the Licchavis on the coins of Chandra Gupta I and Samudra Gupta, and the fact that the Licchavis had ceased to exist in India by that time, are adduced as supportive evidence. Bhūmi Varman, the successor of Bhāskara Varman, he identifies as a contemporary of Chandra Gupta I and Vṛṣadeva as that of his son Samudra Gupta.[3] Through this rather clever, but questionable manipulation, Dr. Regmi cuts down the list of sixteen or seventeen kings in the chronicles to a handier four or five. This also brings the ancient history of Nepal down to Vṛṣadeva, the Licchavi ruler who is mentioned in the later inscriptions. The matter is then further simplified by regarding Jaya Varman on Kirkpatrick's list as Jayadeva I of the Pashupati inscription of Jayadeva II.

This inscription set up by King Jayadeva II in A. D. 733 within the precincts of the Pashupatinath temple gives a list of kings which is no less imaginative in its approach and conception than that of the chronicles themselves. The chronology of the dynasty starts with the sun-god, moves through a list of mythical or Pauranic rulers like Manu, Ikṣvāku, Vikukṣi, Viśvagaśva, Sagara, Dilīpa and Asamañjasa, and finally proceeds to a ruler called Supuṣpa, remotely identifiable with Paśupuṣpa Deva on Kirkpatrick's genealogical list. We are told further by the inscription that names of some of the rulers before Supuṣpa have been omitted, and that even after Supuṣpa some twenty names have been left out before the name of Vṛṣadeva appears. Vṛṣadeva is followed by Saṅkaradeva and Dharmadeva, after whom the rule of his son and successor, Mānadeva I commences. The Changunarayan inscription of Mānadeva I (dated A.D. 464) begins the roll of the Licchavi kings with Vṛṣadeva.

There was, for some time, a good deal of controversy about the dates used in the inscriptions of Mānadeva I and his successors. His inscription at Changunarayan is dated in the year 386, and the succeeding inscriptions follow serially down to the time of Aṃśuvarman when a new era is introduced. According to Bhagavanlal Indraji, who was the first to publish Licchavi inscriptions, the earlier dates used by the Licchavis belonged to the Vikram era, which began in the year 57 B.C. On the mistaken notion that it was the Vikram era which was employed in Nepal during the Licchavi period some historians concluded that the country was under the control of the Imperial Guptas. In his introduction to the *Gupta Inscriptions* and in his article in *Indian Antiquary* of July 1886, J. F. Fleet sought to attribute the Licchavi inscriptions in Nepal to the Gupta era, which began in A.D. 320. Sylvain Levi regarded the dates as belonging to an era unique to Nepal commencing in A.D.110. R. G. Basak, author of *History of North Eastern India*, like Bhagavanlal Indraji, considered the dates up to the time of Śivadeva as Vikram Era dates. However, like Fleet, he regarded the dates on Śivadeva I's inscriptions as relating to the Gupta era, probably because he read 300 on one of Śivadeva's inscriptions for what other scholars had deciphered as 500. However, Dr. R. C. Majumdar, in his article on the chronology of the early kings of Nepal, convincingly demonstrated that the dates on the Licchavi inscriptions up to the time of Aṃśuvarman's emergence as an absolute ruler, belong to the Śaka era, which began in A.D. 78.[4] This is now accepted by all scholars.

The existence of the Licchavis as a political power prior to the rise of Mānadeva cannot be denied, because the marriage of a Licchavi princess to Chandra Gupta I, at the close of the third century A.D., served to enhance the power of the Imperial Gupta dynasty of India. However, it still remains to be proved that the Licchavi princess, Kumārī Devī, whom Chandra Gupta I married belonged to the Licchavi ruling house of Nepal.

The controversy about the supposed supremacy in Nepal of Samudra Gupta, Chandra Gupta's son, is also still to be settled. According to some historians, Nepal must have acknowledged the suzerainty of the Gupta empire under Samudra Gupta because Nepal is mentioned among his tributaries. Other historians are of the opinion that Samudra Gupta mentioned Nepal not as one of his tributaries but as one of those frontier kingdoms that maintained friendly relations with him.[5] It seems likely that Nepal was not a colony of the Guptas in the ordinary sense of the word, although it may have acknowledged the nominal suzerainty of the Gupta Empire when this was at its zenith.

Mānadeva I

With Mānadeva I we move on to the *terra firma* of history supported by epigraphic and numismatic evidence. Mānadeva I was the first Nepali King who left behind him inscriptions and coins. His inscription on the Changunarayan pillar, at Changu about six miles to the northeast of Kathmandu, is the earliest historical inscription with a date so far available in Nepal. Fourteen inscriptions of Mānadeva's reign have been found, and they cover a period of forty-one years, from A.D. 464 to 505.

If what the inscriptions state about Mānadeva I is to be believed, he impressed everyone with a pleasant smiling manner that inspired confidence in his visitors. He was as talented as he was handsome. He loved his subjects and looked after the poor. He was highly devoted to his mother, Rājyavatī, who did not burn herself with her dead husband but chose to assist her son, Mānadeva, in administering the country.

Mānadeva was brave and resolute. He had learned the science of warfare in battles fought at his father's side. After his father's death, he went to war with the rebel feudatories, first in the east, and then conquered Mallapuri on the bank of a river to the west. According to some writers, the Mallapuri that Mānadeva I conquered was probably what is now modern Kasia and Pava in the Gorakhpur district of the Indian state of Uttar Pradesh. According to others, the Mallapuri mentioned in Mānadeva's inscription refers to the land of the Mallas in the western hill area of Nepal, either in the Gandaki or Karnali basin.[6]

Mānadeva was a devotee of Vishnu and set up two images of his favourite god in the extended posture (*vikrānta*) which are among the specimens of Licchavi sculpture which have come down to us intact. Like other Licchavi kings, he had a liberal outlook on religion. Although he himself believed in the worship of Vishnu, his wives set up Shivalingas, the pillars representing the phallus of Shiva, and probably practised Shaivism. Mānadeva himself set up a Shivalinga near the Vishnumati river in 474. Buddhism existed side by side with Vaishnavism, Shaivism and the Śhākta cult. The Buddhist monastery of Māna Vihāra, evidently named after Mānadeva, is thought to have been built on his orders. There are indications that this Māna Vihāra was situated at Swayambhu.

Mānadeva put up a huge building called Mānagṛha, which probably served both as his personal residence as well as the official seat of his government. He also put into circulation coins known as *mānāṅkas* which bear the name of his queen, Bhoginī.

Mānadeva was a powerful monarch who suppressed the feudatories with a strong hand. Probably these had grown aggressive and defiant in scattered pockets of Nepal after the death of his father, as was the case in India after the Licchavi republic of Vaishali was incorporated into the Magadhan empire by Ajātaśatru. The gradual emergence of regents like Aṃśuvarman and the Gupta co-rulers during the period of Mānadeva's successors shows that the Licchavi monarchy in Nepal later had to face a renewed challenge from the feudatories.

Mānadeva's Successors

Mānadeva was succeeded by his son, Mahīdeva. Since both the last inscription of Mānadeva I and the first inscription of Vasantadeva, Mahīdeva's successor, are dated A.D. 506, Mahīdeva must have reigned only a few months.

Nine inscriptions of Vasantadeva's reign are available. It appears from some of these inscriptions that the feudatories with the Gupta name-endings had begun to emerge as leading figures. The Thankot

Ādinārāyāṇa inscription of Vasantadeva mentions Virocana Gupta as 'Performer of Sacrifices' (*yājñika*), but Vasantadeva's Lagantol inscription contains the name of Ravi Gupta who is called 'Commander-in-chief and Chamberlain' (*sarvadaṇḍanāyaka mahā-pratihāra*). The Balambu inscription of Vasantadeva mentions one Kramalila as 'Feudal Overlord' (*mahārāja mahāsāmanta*). Other inscriptions of Vasantadeva reveal that the Guptas were quite prominent and exercised considerable authority during Vasantadeva's reign. As the last of the nine inscriptions of Vasantadeva is dated A.D. 532 and the next dated inscription (at least two reigns later) is of 538, it is difficult to ascertain how long he actually ruled.

On the basis of the evidence of coins called *guṇāṅkas*, which resemble, in many respects, the coins of Mānadeva I, known as *mānāṅkas*, the name of a new king, Guṇakāmadeva, has been brought in at about this time. However, further research is needed to prove his place and identity in the established line of the Licchavi rulers.

It is not clear whether Vasantadeva was succeeded by Manudeva or Vāmandeva, but an inscription found near Sankhu tells us that Vāmanadeva was ruling in A.D. 538. Rāmadeva ascended the throne after Vāmanadeva. One of his two inscriptions shows that he was reigning in A.D. 545.

Rāmadeva was followed by Gaṇadeva, whose reign had commenced by A.D. 557. He has been assigned a reign of at least eight years as his last dated inscription is A.D. 565. Gaṅgadeva has now been found to have been Gaṇadeva's successor and the immediate predecessor of Mānadeva II. Mānadeva II is now credited with the founding of a new era, beginning in A.D. 576, which was hitherto attributed to Aṃśuvarman, the co-ruler and successor of Śivadeva I.

Śivadeva I and Aṃśuvarman

Sixteen inscriptions of Śivadeva's reign throw considerable light on the Licchavi period. His inscriptions cover a period of fourteen years from A.D. 590 to 604. The Guptas seem to have temporarily ceased to be the rivals of the ruling authority of the Licchavi king. At this point opposition came from Aṃśuvarman, who is said to have belonged to the Vaiṣya Ṭhakurī clan and who started out as an influential officer of Śivadeva's court but in time rose to be a co-ruler. Finally, he became more important than the legitimate ruler, Śivadeva himself, and succeeded him after his death.

It is erroneously believed that the system of twin kingdoms or *dvairajya* appeared for the first time in Nepal's history during this period. However, as there was no territorial division, the Aṃśuvarman- - Licchavi relation was actually more like the Shah—Rana type of dual authority in modern times with two rulers ruling one and the same territory as Mahārājadhirāja and Mahārāja from 1856 through 1950.

To turn to Aṃśuvarman's reign in Nepal: he is mentioned as feudatory (*sāmanta*) in the beginning and then as chief feudatory (*mahāsāmanta*). However, an inscription toward the end of Śivadeva's reign describes him as King of Kings and the Feudal Overlord (*mahārājadhirāja śrī sāmanta*). It is difficult to determine exactly when Aṃśuvarman's absolute rule commenced, and this task is complicated by his introduction of the Mānadeva II era into the inscriptions without identifying the era. This led some scholars down the wrong path. Sylvain Levi identifies it with the Tibetan era, and according to him the dawn of the Tibetan era in Nepal coincided with Aṃśuvarman's acceptance of Tibetan suzerainty. Levi has confused the Mānadeva II era with the Tibetan era and wrongly concluded that Nepal came under Tibet's domination. Similarly, scholars like Bhagavanlal Indraji, J. F. Fleet and F. Kielhorn have confused the Mānadeva II era in Nepal with the Harṣa era of India and have erroneously inferred that Nepal came under the sway of Harṣa's empire. While sharing the confusion of the aforementioned scholars, Prof. N. N. Ghosh does not, however, endorse their conclusion that Nepal was a part of Harṣa's empire.[7]

Aṃśuvarman's inscriptions cover a period of sixteen years from the 29th year (A.D. 605) to the 45th year (A.D. 621) of the Mānadeva II era. On the basis of the length of time covered by his inscriptions, he may have ruled on his own for sixteen years. His inscriptions after the 39th year of the Mānadeva era (A.D. 615) refer to him as *śrī*. Coins also bear his name, *śrī aṃśu*, on one side and the title mahārājadhirāja on the other. It redounds to the credit of Aṃśuvarman that the royal title "The Most Venerable King of Kings' (*paramabhaṭṭāraka mahārājadhirāja* assumed by him was also adopted after him by each of the Licchavi rulers, and the era introduced by him was also followed by his successors to the end of the Licchavi period.

Evaluation of Aṃśuvarman's Rule

Aṃśuvarman's reign was characterized by great architectural and sculptural achievements. Like Mānadeva I , Aṃśuvarman built a beautiful palace, called Kailāskūṭa Bhavana, which served both as his personal residence and the official seat of his government. Many fountains for drinking water and water conduits were built during his reign, some of which are still in existence. Aṃśuvarman also put up many Shivalingas, or pillars and images of Shiva.

The famous seventh-century Chinese traveller, Hsuan Chuang (Hsuan- tsang) mentions Aṃśuvarman in the account of his travels in India as the king of Nepal who had reigned shortly before the journey of which he writes. He says that Aṃśuvarman was renowned for his bravery, learning and piety.

From his inscriptions also, it appears that Aṃśuvarman was a man of learning as well as action. In addition to fighting victoriously against his rival feudatories in many battles, he was well read and had a deep respect for other scholars.

Aṃśuvarman was a man of religious temperament and was constantly engaged in the study of religious books. Because he had a profound knowledge of religious lore, he was eager to make sure that temples and monasteries were properly maintained. He therefore set up generous trusts to meet their expenses.

Although Aṃśuvarman believed in Shaivism and adopted the title 'He Who Meditates at the Feet of the Most Venerable Pashupati' *paśupatibhaṭṭāraka pādānudhyāta* to prove his devotion to Shiva, he also assisted the Vaishnava and Buddhist institutions. He was a generous and liberal king, treating Hindus and Buddhists alike without discrimination and a benevolent monarch who wrote on one of his inscriptions: 'I am always thinking of how I can make my people happy'.

Aṃśuvarman did not belong to the Licchavi dynasty, yet in all probability, he adopted Śivadeva's son, Udayadeva, as his heir. One of Aṃśuvarman's inscriptions refers to Udayadeva as 'Crown Prince' (yuvarāja) and 'Witness' (*dūtaka*) [to the edict].

Aṃśuvarman's Successors—Re-emergence of the Gupta Co-rulers

Aṃśuvarman was indeed followed by Udayadeva, one of whose inscriptions have survived, but it was a short reign of at most three years. An inscription of A.D. 623 presents us with the dual government of Dhruvadeva, a Licchavi and probably a brother or cousin of Udayadeva, and Jiṣṇu Gupta, a member of the influential family of the Guptas. It was the kind of government for which Aṃśuvarman had set a precedent. There is evidence that Udayadeva had been ousted, but nothing is known about the circumstances that led to the ousting of Udayadeva and the emergence of a Gupta co-ruler. Probably the Guptas began to raise their heads again when the strong man, Aṃśuvarman who had suppressed them, disappeared from the scene. It is possible that Udayadeva was removed from the throne by Dhruvadeva after a short reign with the assistance of the influential family of the Guptas. According to the T'ang annals, Udayadeva's son, Narendradeva, fled the country after his father was dethroned by his uncle, sought asylum in Tibet and later regained his ancestral throne with the help of Tibetan authorities.[8]

According to a popular Tibetan legend, there was a Nepali king called Go Cha, whom Sylvain Levi identified as Udayavarman on the basis of the literal meaning of the Tibetan word. Popular legend has it that this king had a daughter by the name of Bri-btsumn or Bhṛkuti, whom Song-tsen Gampo, the famous king of Tibet, married. But Dr. G. Tucci has shown in his article 'The Wives of *Srong-btsan-sgam-po*' in *Oriens Extremus*, 1962, that the Tibetan king's marriage to a Nepali princess is almost certainly a legend without historical basis. Thanks to the attention and prominence this story received from scholars like Levi, it was for quite some time accepted as an historical fact.

Five inscriptions of the joint rule of Dhruvadeva and Jiṣṇu Gupta have survived. The dates are legible on only two of the inscriptions which are dated 48 and 49 of the Mānadeva II era, corresponding to A.D. 624 and 625. The dual government of Dhruvadeva and Jiṣṇu Gupta was followed by Jiṣṇu Gupta's absolute rule, which was soon replaced by the dual government of Bhīmārjunadeva and Jiṣṇu Gupta. Three inscriptions of this government have come to light. The dates (which can be read on only two of them) are 55 and 57 of the Mānadeva II Era, corresponding to A.D. 631 and 633.

The dual government of Bhīmārjunadeva and Jiṣṇu Gupta was superseded by that of Bhīmārjunadeva and Viṣṇu Gupta, the latter acquiring authority from his father, Jiṣṇu Gupta, to rule in his name. The inscriptions available for this joint rule are dated A.D. 640 and 641.

Narendradeva

It was from Bhīmārjunadeva and Viṣṇu Gupta that Narendradeva wrested his ancestral throne with the help of Tibet. The Chinese annals do not describe in detail the circumstances of Narendradeva's return to power. They are content merely to mention his escape to Tibet after the dethronement of his father and his subsequent recovery of the throne with the assistance of the Tibetan government.

By the seventh century A.D. Tibet had emerged as a powerful kingdom with Lhasa as its capital. This had the effect of transforming Kathmandu, a remote and isolated valley in the sub-Himalayan region, into a cultural and commercial centre and a bridge between South Asia and Central Asia. Limited trade may have taken place across the Himalaya via Kathmandu even before this, but it was only in the seventh century A.D. that political relations gained importance.

At the time that Hsuang Chuang and his party were returning to China by way of the Pamirs, a Chinese mission of twenty-two men, led by Li I-piao and Wang Hsuan Tse, was proceeding towards India by a new route, which had never before been used for the journey between Nepal and China via Lhasa. South-west of Lhasa it reached the Himalaya and crossed the Kerung pass. The opening of this route must have greatly stimulated the growth of commercial and cultural intercourse between these countries, since the early Chinese pilgrims to India, like Fa-Hsien and Hsuang Chuang, had preferred the great length and the hazards of a journey across the Gobi Desert and the Hindukush to the risks encountered by crossing the Tibetan plateau and the high Himalaya.

Narendradeva takes his place among the leading personalities of the Licchavi period, like Mānadeva I and Aṃśuvarman. Thirteen inscriptions of Narendradeva's reign are available covering the period from A.D. 643 to 679, and we also have Chinese sources of information about him:

> Seated on the throne is Narendradeva, bedecked with diamonds, pearls and other jewels, wearing earrings of gold and with an amulet of Buddha's likeness dangling on his breast. In the midst of his court, men sprinkle scented water and scatter flowers. On the king's right and left, courtiers are seated on the floor. Behind the throne, countless soldiers stand at arms.[9]

Such is the description of Narendradeva and his court given in the Chinese annals, based on the account of Wang Hsuan T'se. Narendradeva's reign reflected the glorious achievements of the Licchavi period in general.

Narendradeva must have heard glowing descriptions of the wealth and splendour in the Imperial Court of China during his stay in Tibet as a refugee. Chinese and Tibetan annals state that the early Tibetan ruler, Song-tsen Gampo, wielded some authority over the Kathmandu Valley, reportedly for having helped King Narendradeva and his family recover the throne that had been lost two decades earlier. Narendradeva initiated formal relations between Nepal and China. He sent a mission to China with all kinds of gifts and succeeded in establishing cordial relations with the Chinese court.

A few years before Narendradeva's reign, King Harṣvardhana had ruled in northern India. He had established friendly relations with China, and there was a regular exchange of emissaries between the two countries. After Harṣvardhana's death, an envoy from China, Wang Hsuan T'se, arrived in India with a large entourage. The envoy was attacked by Arjuna ('Arlo-nashun' in the Chinese text), who had usurped the throne after Harṣvardhana's death. Arjuna put some of the emissaries to death, sent others to prison, and confiscated the gifts they had brought. Wang Hsuan T'se and one of his colleagues managed to escape and reached Narendradeva's palace in Nepal.

Narendradeva, the king of Nepal, and Song-tsen Gampo, the king of Tibet, helped the Chinese emissaries to attack the impetuous Arjuna by putting troops at their disposal. Narendradeva sent seven thousand cavalrymen to the aid of the Chinese ambassador, who led an assault on the usurper, captured him with his family and carried them off to China.

Friendship between Nepal and China was thus firmly established. China was grateful to Nepal for its help in this crisis and for the vindication of its honour. A few years later, the same Chinese ambassador again passed through Nepal on his way to visit centres of Buddhist pilgrimage in India.

At the time of Narendradeva, Nepal was a prosperous and powerful country. The contemporary descriptions of the grandeur of the royal court attest to this. Narendradeva's palace, called Bhadrādhivāsa, was beautiful and majestic. According to a description in the Chinese annals, it was a seven-storyed building roofed with plates of copper. Its metal work, balustrades, screens and beams were decorated with semi-precious stones, and in the four corners of the ground floor were crocodile heads of gold with water flowing from their mouths in a continuous stream.

In the days of Narendradeva, the Nepali people lived in houses of wood. Their walls were painted in bright colours and decorated with murals and friezes. The people were very fond of festivals and celebrated them by playing a great variety of native instruments. Wrestling and bullfights were popular forms of entertainment. Bullfights were a special feature of religious functions that usually attracted large gatherings of people. Religious processions (*jātrās*) were not unknown, but they had not gained the same prominence they acquired later during the Malla period.

Narendradeva adopted the same royal title (*paramabhaṭṭāraka mahārājadhirāja*) as Aṃśuvarman and showed devotion to Shiva. The beginning of the annual festival of the image of the god Lokesvara--Matsyendranātha is associated with his reign. Most of his inscriptions bear the Buddhist Wheel of Religion (*dharmacakra*) flanked by two deer, but some of his inscriptions also display the traditional Shaiva and Vaishnava symbols of the bull and the conch with Vishnu's wheel (*cakra*).

At that time Sanṣkrit was the medium of higher education and Sanskrit learning was fairly widespread among the people. Some of them were well-versed in astrology and astronomy and could draw up calendars on the basis of calculations of the various phases of the moon. Since artistic and literary refinement presuppose a certain level of material prosperity, Nepal must have enjoyed a fairly high standard of agricultural and commercial development.

The country had by now become a thriving centre by serving as a gateway from India to China, both for merchandise and for scholars who disseminated knowledge and culture as they travelled. About this time Nepal learned from China the art of paper making. Handmade paper of the finest quality was added to its traditional exports of musk, orpiment, blankets and other woollen goods to India.

Śivadeva II

According to a Buddhist legend, Narendradeva retired to a monastery in his old age. He was succeeded on the throne by Śivadeva II. Seven inscriptions of his reign have come down to us and they cover a period of perhaps sixteen years from A.D. 685 to 701.

Śivadeva II, described in his son's inscription as one who 'by his glory put to shame all hostile kings', sought to enhance the prestige of his family by marrying the daughter of Bhogavarman, the Maukhari king in the plains. Śivadeva II's wife's name is given as Vatsadevī and she is further identified as the granddaughter of Adityasena, King of Magadha.

Although Śivedeva II, like his predecessors, was devoted to Shiva, he saw to it that the deities of Mahāyāna Buddhism were not neglected and that Buddhist monasteries were properly looked after. He also continued the tradition of his predecessors in administration and trade and made sure that Nepal was not cut off from the mainstream of Hindu culture.

Jayadeva II and His Successors

Śivadeva II's son and successor was Jayadeva II. At least six inscriptions from his reign have come to light. All but one of them are partially damaged. Those which do have dates give us a span of twenty years from A.D. 713 to 733. As noted above, Jayadeva's inscription at Pashupatinath gives a chronology of the Licchavi rulers. Some regard the inscriptions of Jayadeva II as the last recorded inscriptions of the Licchavi period.

Jayadeva II continued his father's policy of marrying into the family of the rulers in the plains and married the daughter of the king of Gauḍa. As the *kṣatriyas* of the plains had long considered the Licchavis to be an inferior kind of *kṣatriya*, the marriages of Śivadeva and Jayadeva II to the daughters of the *kṣatriya* kings of the plains acquired an additional importance.

One of Jayadeva II's inscriptions mentions Vijayadeva as his heir apparent, and the chronicles add a few more names after him. For a long time nothing of substance was known about the Licchavi period after Jayadeva II. The period between his death and the rise of Rāghavadeva, the founder of the Nepal Era (*saṃvat*), was described as the dark period of Nepali history. Historians experienced real difficulty in filling up the gap between Jayadeva II and Rāghavadeva and usually furnished four or five names of kings from the available genealogical lists with possible suggestions about regnal years to fill up the gap. However, an inscription of one Śivadeva (III) dated 174 of the Mānadeva II era (i.e. A.D. 750) has recently come to light. This places him immediately before Mānadeva III, whose sole inscription is dated 180 of the Mānadeva II era (A.D. 756), and who was followed by Gaṇadeva II. Two recent discoveries give a Baliraja ruling in 250 (A.D. 826) and a Baladeva ruling in 271 (A.D. 847). A manuscript dated 301 of the Mānadeva II era attests to the reign at that time of another Mānadeva. If this Mānadeva IV is dated about 875, in accordance with Dr. J. C. Regmi's suggestion, there is little gap to be filled up between this date and A.D. 879 when Rāghavadeva began to rule.[10]

Nepal's Political Status and Territorial Extent

A word may be appropriate at this stage about Nepal having been Tibet's vassal for quite sometime following the rule of the Tibetan King Song-tsen Gampo. Popular legends assume, without basis in fact, that the defeat of Aṃśuvarman by Song-tsen Gampo preceded the marriage of the Nepali Princess Bribtsum, or Bhṛkuti, to the Tibetan king. Again the widely held view of a so-called 'Tibetan Era' (A.D. 595) in Nepal, an invention of Sylvain Levi, has absolutely no factual basis, and therefore cannot be cited as proof of Tibetan suzerainty or domination over Nepal.

However, there can be no cogent reason against Tibetan suzerainty (but not domination) over Nepal for a certain period of time, if we take into account the Chinese and Tibetan Records. The *Ch'in-tand-shu* (*Old History of the T'ang Dynasty*) and the valuable Tibetan documents found at Tunhuang (containing a chronology of events in Tibet from A.D. 650 to 747) state that Tibetan kings very often stayed in Nepali territory as if it were part of their kingdom. It appears that, in return for the help Narendradeva received from the Tibetans in regaining his throne, he had to make certain concessions to them.[11]

It is difficult to define precisely the geographical and political boundaries of Nepal during the Licchavi period. Some claim that Mānadeva I 's suppression of the feudatory rebels in the east probably meant the incorporation into his kingdom of the area of the Kirātas which might have extended as far as the eastern limits of the present kingdom of Nepal, if not beyond it. An Indian scholar is of the opinion that Nepal's eastern and south-eastern boundaries at one time may have touched the limits of Kamarupa or Upper Assam in the hills, and those of Dawak (Naugaun) in the plains. Dawak terminated in the territory of the modern district of Jalpaiguri in West Bengal.

Mānadeva I was credited with the conquest of Mallapuri in the west. Some authors think that the Mallapuri Mānadeva I conquered, did not refer to Pava and Kasia in the west but to the territory of the Khasa Mallas in the Karnali basin, which extended as far as Kartripur or modern Garhwal.[12]

However, this is speculation on the basis of very little evidence and in his latest work on Ancient Nepal, Dr. Dilli Raman Regmi considers all the theories that have been propounded and concludes:

> To sum up, Nepal [in the Ancient Period] was situated over the hilly region extending west to east from the river Budhi Gandak to the river Sunkosi and a little further. The actual line probably lay between the river Trisuli Gandak in the west and the confluence of the Sunkosi and Rosi in the east. The northern line probably touched the snowy ranges of the Himalayas. There could be confusion as to the southern boundary. In all probability the boundary might lie along the Churia [Chure] ranges.[13]

The Licchavi era is followed by a dark period in Nepal's history which lasted for about two centuries. This has led some scholars to assume that Nepal must have fallen under foreign domination of some kind during this time. Whatever may be the facts, there is no doubt that Nepal suffered a decline in territory and power at this juncture.

NOTES

1. Colonel Kirkpatrick, *An Account of the Kingdom of Nepaul*, (1811), Reprint: New Delhi, Manjusri Publishing House, 1969. p. 259.
2. D.R. Regmi, *Ancient Nepal*, Calcutta, Firma K.L. Mukhopadhyay, 1960, p. 70.
3. *Ibid.*, p. 71-72.
4. R.C. Majumdar, 'The Eras in Nepal,' *Journal of the Asiatic Society* (1959) I:1, 47-49.
5. D.R. Regmi, *Ancient Nepal*, p. 127.
6. *Ibid.*, p. 131-35.
7. N.N. Ghosh, *Early History of India*, Allahabad, p. 316.
8. D.R. Regmi, *Ancient Nepal*, p. 177.
9. *Ibid.*
10. Jagadish Candra Regmi, *Prācin Nepālko Rājnītik Itihās*, Kathmandu, Royal Nepal Academy, V.S. 2035, 178-79.
11. D.R. Regmi, *Ancient Nepal*, p.151.
12. *Ibid.*, p. 106-7.,
13. Dilli Raman Regmi, *Inscriptions of Ancient Nepal*, Vol. 1. New Delhi, Abhinav Publications, 1983, p.17.

CHAPTER III

LICCHAVI SOCIETY

The Licchavi dynasty, like the Malla and the Shah dynasties of a later period in Nepal's history, was founded by immigrants from India who came to Nepal to escape political persecution in the country of their origin. The last known home of the Licchavis was the republic of Vaishali in the Muzaffarpur, Champaran and Darbhanga districts of North Bihar in India. The ancestors of the Licchavi rulers in Nepal were first displaced by the invasion of their republic by the expanding empire of Magadha and subsequently by the Kuśāna emperors. By the time the rule of the Licchavi dynasty began in Nepal, not only the Licchavi republic of Vaishali, but also the Śākya republic of Kapilavastu and the Videha republic of Mithila, in the areas adjoining Nepal, had already disappeared under the impact of new historical trends and forces released in the wake of rigorous empire building in India.

Politics and Administration

In the plains the Licchavis were known for their republican tradition, but in Nepal they founded a strong monarchy to hold in check the divisive forces of feudalism. Local conditions in Nepal at times necessitated the unique system of dual government described earlier. This does not mean, however, that the Licchavis completely abandoned their republican tradition in Nepal. They initiated a limited measure of local self-government by introducing an institution known as *pāñcālī*. The *pāñcālīs* were representative committees of the village responsible for the administration of local affairs and the collection of the kings' taxes. The members of the *pāñcālī* committees were called *pāñcālīkas*. Autonomous bodies or trusts known as *goṣṭhī*, reminiscent of the *gūṭhīs* in the later periods of Nepal's history, administered private and public trusts of different kinds. A member of one of these trusts was known as *gauṣṭhika*. Hence a participant or participatory system of government by committees and conferences was not entirely unknown in Nepal under the Licchavis.

On the other hand, these institutions of local self-government in Nepal were not allowed to affect the absolute power of the Licchavi monarchs and their co-rulers in any way. The inscriptions state clearly that the king's command was a law unto the people and whoever disobeyed it would be very strictly dealt with.

The administration of the state was fairly well-organised. The smallest unit of administration was the village (*grāma*) and the largest unit was probably the province (*pradeśa*). Between them there were intermediate territorial and administrative units such as the city (*pūra*), *tala, draṅga, janapada, koṭṭa*, all of which implied a graded collection of villages or a city. Government departments and legal offices were in all probability called *adhikaraṇa* and *karaṇa.*

The king who was called 'The Revered King of Kings' (*bhaṭṭāraka mahārājadhirāja*) was the highest executive officer of the state. Monarchy was based on some kind of theory of divine right, as the monarch claimed to rule over his fellow beings as an incarnation of Narayana and by the favour of Lord Pashupati or Shiva. Unlike that of some of the republican peoples, such as the Śākyas who had an elected monarchy, the Licchavi monarchy in Nepal was purely hereditary. The next office in the hierarchy of the state was that of the crown prince (*yuvarāja*) and he often appeared as witness (*dūtaka*) to the royal inscriptions. The king's other sons and relatives performed such state duties as witnesses to royal acts (*dūtaka*), commanders of the army (*baladhyakṣya*) or state counsellors (*vārtta*). Since justice and morality were associated with religion, the judges of the civil and criminal courts were called 'Religious-authorities' (*dharmādhikāra*), and the state minister for religious affairs was known as *dharmārajikāmātya*. Other important members of the official hierarchy mentioned in the Licchavi inscriptions are the Minister of the Crown Prince (*kumāramātya*), the Chamberlain of the Palace (*pratihāra*), the Commander in Chief who was also responsible for imposing penalties for legal and state offences (*sarvadaṇḍanāyaka pratihāra*). Lesser officials such as *adhikṛta*, *ayukta*, *daṇḍanāyaka*, *dauvārika*, are also mentioned. Though the precise functions of these officials are not known, the specific names indicate that there was a classification of their functions and duties and that the government machinery was well integrated. In our present state of knowledge we cannot elaborate on the actual working of the state machinery.[1]

Economic Conditions

The people of Nepal were a prosperous agricultural and trading community during the Licchavi period. Land and agriculture were the main bases of the economy. Inscriptions yield information about two land measures in use at the time: *bhūmi* and *mānika*. The present day Newari *bhū*, which is equivalent to two acres of land, is probably derived from the *bhūmi* of the Licchavi period. Government officers and public institutions, monasteries and temples depended on income from land-grants for their support. The main function of the popular village committees or *goṣṭhis* seems to have been the support of religious leaders and religious rituals (*bhagavad vāśudeva brāhmaṇa gosthi, indra g., dhvaja g., pradīpa g., dhūpa g.*, etc.). Though some of them provided support for more social works such as the 'Water Supply Committee' (*pāniya praṇālī g.*), it is not clear from the inscriptions whether they were used for all-round village development.

Taxes of various kinds are mentioned. The king received his share: one sixth, one-eighth or one-twelfth of the agriculture produce from the land, depending on the productivity of the land. This tax was known as *bhāga-bhoga-kara*. In addition to land revenue, taxes either in kind or in cash were levied on such things as jars of oil, earthen pots, firewood, textiles, onions and garlic, fish and animals like pigs and sheep. Except in one or two cases the rate of taxation is not known. A tax of one *kārṣāpaṇa* was levied on rams and later reduced to four *paṇas*. (One *kārṣāpaṇa* was equal to sixteen copper *paṇas*). Two kinds of forced labour are mentioned (*bhoṭṭa viṣṭi and phalanju viṣṭi*). What this forced labour was used for is not clear except that the first certainly involved porterage.[2]

At this time Nepal was also a thriving centre for trade and handicrafts. It was involved in the profitable entrepot trade between India and Tibet. Waterproof blankets of a black colour from Nepal, known as *bhiṅgī*, were prized in India, and handmade paper from Nepal was India's choice import. Other imports included musk and orpiment. The prevalence of a tax known as the 'Indigo Tax' (*nailyakara*) indicates that dyeing was a home industry of some kind. The merchants or commercial class must have been quite affluent as is shown by an inscription of the time of Mānadeva I. The inscription on the pedestal of an image of the sun-god mentions one Guhamitra as the leader of the business community. Trading was certainly not considered to be a disreputable profession.

The Licchavi period has yielded a variety of coins, though they are limited in quantity. Mānadeva I was the first to circulate his own coins called *mānāṅkas* with a lion on the obverse and an image of the goddess Lakshmi on the reverse. The next group of coins that has come to light comprises coins known as *guṇāṅkas* which bear a female image on the obverse and an elephant on the reverse. According to the Nepali historian Baburam Acarya, the *guṇāṅka* coins were struck by Mānadeva I himself. However, some other Nepali historians have, on the basis of these coins, posited a king by the name of Guṇakāmadeva who possibly succeeded Gạnadeva. Aṃśuvarman's coins bear the the image of lions in different postures and sometimes with wings. The coin of a lesser ruler, Jiṣṇu Gupta, is of high artistic merit and bears the image of a winged horse, or possibly lion, with a trident which looks like a thunderbolt. Other coins of the Licchavi period called *paśupati* and *vaiśravaṇa* coins are not named after any kings. They yield a rich variety of iconographic features. Some writers have pointed out a similarity between the Licchavi coins and the Kuśāna, Yaudheya and Gupta coins. However these latter have no real resemblance to the former. Unlike the Indian coins, the Licchavi coins do not bear any monograph or mint-marks but are punch-marked. They also differ vastly in iconographic features except for the common gods and goddesses of the Hindu pantheon like Laksmi, Shiva and Kuvera and some of the fixed traditional symbols associated with each of these. So far only copper coins from the Licchavi period have been discovered, but inscriptions give indications that gold and silver coins were also in circulation during the Licchavi period. The standard measures of money or currency in use were: *kārṣāpaṇa*, *purāṇa*, *paṇa*, *paṇapurṇa*. One *kārṣāpaṇa* was equivalent to sixteen *paṇas*.

Social and Religious Conditions

The Licchavis were considered to be an inferior kind of Ksatriya by the 'pure' Kṣatiryas in the plains. The indigenous people of Nepal were originally a non-Hindu, casteless community which, initially subject to Shaiva and Vaishnava influence, was eventually overwhelmed by the influence of Mahāyāna Buddhism from the India of the Kuśānas just before the advent of the Licchavis. The caste system, based on the four classes (*varṇa*) or broad classifications of labour in society did not make much headway in Licchavi Nepal among these people. However, some ambitious kings like Aṃśuvarman, Śivadeva II and Jayadeva II tried their best to enforce the rule of occupation according to the caste of the people.

Men and women enjoyed equal status in performing religious and social duties. Women also set up religious trusts and images as their tribute to the memory of their deceased relatives. Since even widows made donations of land for religious purposes in their own names, it would appear that women possessed the right to landed property. Polygamy was prevalent among the upper classes and the rulers. Mānadeva I had three wives who each followed their own inclinations in matters of religious worship. *Satī*, or the practice of burning oneself with the dead body of one's husband, was not entirely unknown, but was rarely performed. Mānadeva's mother, Rājyavatī, herself did not perform *satī* after her husband, King Dharmadeva, died. Inscriptions reveal instances of widow remarriage and divorce. Among the poorer people, women publicly worked for a living. The women of the well-to-do classes were probably educated, since one of the inscriptions refers to Mānadeva's daughter as having been 'proficient in all arts'. Men devoted to the pursuit of knowledge were patronised through a public institution called *agrahara* supported by tax-free property and managed by organizations of Brahman scholars or Buddhist monks (*āryabhikṣu saṅgha*).

The earliest settlers in the Kathmandu valley were a non-Aryan people as attested to by the large number of places in the Licchavi inscriptions with non-Sanskrit names. The still current Newari names for the three cities of the Valley: Yẽ (Kathmandu), Yala (Patan), Khopva (Bhaktapur) trace their origins back to this early period. In the chronicles the Kiratas, who are supposed to be the first people to exercise supremacy in the Valley, have non-Aryan names such as Stangko, Yelambar, etc.

The oldest religion of the Kathmandu Valley seems to be related to a non-Aryan cult of the 'Lord of the Animals' (*paśupati*) who later became identified as Shiva. It appears that the earliest people practised a religion closely related to the later cult of the Paśupatas, but unfortunately the relics of the pre-Aryan period have not yet been unearthed, nor is there any reference to them in the inscriptions of the Licchavi period. Therefore, there is so far no way of tracing the growth of the pre-Aryan culture and its assimilation of later elements. Nepal then was subject to the influence of the pre-Aryan cult of Pashupati and subsequently to Māhāyana Buddhism under the Kuśāna influence to the exclusion of the Brahmanical tradition. The Bharasivas and Bakatakas, who ousted the Kuśānas, must have introduced Shaivism in the form of a revival. Shaivism became the prevailing religion because several sects and subsects of the cult of Pashupati had been known in Nepal for a long time.

Although Shaivism was the religion of most of the rulers (with the exception of Mānadeva I, who was personally more devoted to Vishnu), Vaishnavism, Buddhism and the Śakta worship of the cosmic goddess were in vogue. Both the rulers and the people possessed a highly liberal outlook on religion. Aṃśuvarman adopted Shiva or Pashupati as his guardian deity, and his successors to the throne followed the precedent set by him. However, all of them also looked after Buddhist monasteries and nunneries. Religious temples and institutions were not merely the concern of the rulers and the state, even ordinary people took an interest in them.

Hence, during the time of the Licchavis and their successors (ca. A.D. 400-880) Shaivism, Vaishnavism and Buddhism were known in the Valley, but Shaivism was still the prevailing religion. Perhaps Shaivism owed its popularity to its link with the practices of the non-Aryan cult of Pashupati in the distant past. Pashupati has been acknowledged as the guardian deity of the country by every ruler since Aṃśuvarman (A.D. 604-620). Several later sects and subsects of the Paśupata cult, like the Lakulisa Paśupata sect, the Muṇḍaśṛṁkhalika Paśupata sect, the Śṛṁkhalika Paśupata sect and the Dānaśṛṁkhalika Paśupata sect became prevalent in ancient Nepal. Māhāyana Buddhism, with its emphasis on human compassion as manifest in the ideal of the *bodhisattva* who foregoes his state of *nirvāṇa* to be of service to suffering humanity, gradually gained ground over the Hīnāyana or Lesser Vehicle with its stress on cold reason and logic and on purity of character and austerity of life. The Śakta cult, or the worship of the mother goddess, was known even in the Licchavi period. The image of Palanchok Bhagavatī set up by Mānadeva I's wife and also the images of Naxal Bhagavatī, Sobhābhagavati antedate the medieval period of Nepal's history.

The Soma Siddhānta sect, practising moon-Shiva worship was also in vogue prior to the medieval period, but much more popular was the Sūrya Sampradaya, or the sect that practised sun-worship. A stone image of the sun, in the form of Indra, was set up by a person called Guhamitra in the Licchavi period and reminds one of the strong Kuśāna influence.

Vaishnavism, the mild Hindu cult of the worship of Vishnu as the preserver of life and the universe, was also prevalent. Similarity in the devotional aspects of Vaishnavism and Buddhism may have initially combined the followers of these two sects against the Shaivas, or the adherents of the Shaiva cult. The adherents of the Paśupata cult kept long, uncut hair and followed a more vigorous and spectacular life of renunciation, wearing bark garments and sporting long flowing chains of human skulls.

One also notes that the rulers and the general public of the Licchavi period experimented in religious matters. One such example is that of the Hari-Hara cult. An inscription found standing near the Pashupati temple dated A.D. 565 records the installation of a Hari-Hara image by one government officer called Svāmī Vārtta who seems to be closely associated with the then co-ruler Bhāmma Gupta. Such an early example of a Hari-Hara image is not found even in India.

Religious antagonism of any sort was not evident among the adherents of the different religious sects. This can be deduced from the fact that not only father and sons of the same ruling line worshipped deities of the different sects according to their personal preferences, but their wives were themselves free to worship any deity they chose. Temples and monasteries of the Shaiva, Vaishnava and Buddhist sects were subsidised by the rulers without discrimination. Hence tolerance was the policy of the rulers and the general public alike. Nepal was internationally known for this, for it is remarked on by the famous Chinese pilgrim Yuan Chwang in his memoirs.

Architecture

The Licchavi period is known for its architectural and sculptural achievements. Mānadeva I (A.D. 464-505), Aṃśuvarman (A.D. 604-620) and Narendradeva (A.D. 642-678), the three leading rulers of the period, put up magnificent buildings which served both as their personal residences and as the seats of their governments. These public palaces, known as Mānagṛha, Kailāskūṭa Bhavana, and Bhadrādhivāsa Bhavana were built by Mānadeva I, Aṃśuvarman and Narendradeva respectively. No trace of these buildings remains today, and historians do not even agree on the site of these buildings. According to some historians, Mānagṛha was situated at Madhyalākhu near Deopatan in the Pashupatinath area, and Kailāsakūṭa Bhavana at Hadigaun near Tangal in Kathmandu. Others think that Kailāsakuta Bhavana was located between Deopatan and the Pashupatinath temple. While others place Kailāsakuta Bhavana just a short distance south of the present Hanuman Dhoka in Kathmandu. Although these buildings, constructed primarily of brick, mortar and wood, could not stand the wear and tear of nature over the centuries, references to them in contemporary inscriptions and in the T'ang Annals leave no doubt about their existence. The Chinese sources give a detailed description of the artistic and decorative features of Narendradeva's palace, Bhadrādhivāsa.

Sculpture

The indigenous people of the Kathmandu Valley worshipped stones in their natural shapes as divinities. But the numinous stones failed to awaken the visual imagination of the people or inspire in their minds a sense of artistic restraint, proportion and symmetry. The figures and forms of the gods came from India together with the tools and techniques of their manufacture. The rough and unhewn stone was rooted in the soil of the Kathmandu Valley, which was once the bottom of a lake.

Balbala, the legendary hero of agriculture and sculpture in Nepal, was the first person to break ground for the purpose of cultivation. He was also the first to create an image of himself in stone. The legend of Balbala, 'the stutterer', though ignored by the chronicles admirably fits into the misty, pre-agricultural era as Balbala's sad tale shows how reluctant and hesitant the indigenous inhabitants of the Valley were to chip a stone or dig up the soil for fear of violating the mother goddess of earth.

The change from a pastoral life to an agricultural one corresponded to the change from the use of an unhewn stone to that of the complex organization of the relief of a stele or sculpture in the round. This transition is reflected in the legend of Balbala who is said to have lived during the reign of Vṛṣadeva or shortly before that time. According to the legends, Balbala's statue of himself set the fashion for sculpture in Nepal. At the same time, it is said that King Vṛṣadeva, like his ancestors, set up images of the Buddha and of Avalokitēsvara.

Modern research has shown that the change supposedly brought about by Balbala must be dated earlier than the time of Vṛṣadeva and that the early sculptures can be clearly divided into two periods. The first period stretches at least back to the first century A.D. and lasts until the fourth century A.D. The large number of Hindu sculptures of this period show a marked influence of the Mathura-Kuṣāna tradition. Perhaps the best example of the sculpture of this period is the second century B.C. image of Gaja Lakṣmi from Chyasal Tole in Patan. The heavy build of the body, the sash around the loins of the figure, the large amulets and the elephants on the lotus pod are all typical features of Kusana period sculpture.

From the second half of the fourth century these heavy and bulky forms are replaced by the sophisicated and highly stylized lines accentuated by proportion and linear harmony which are recognized as typical of the sculpture of the Licchavi period. Two of the typical images of this later period are the images of Vishnu set up by the King Mānadeva I, both of which are dated A.D. 467. One of these images, which used to be at Lazimpat, is now in the National Museum, Kathmandu, and the other one is at its original site in the area of the Pashupatinath temple. Although these two images bear the same date in their inscriptions, the one in the National Museum is the more elegant and sophisticated of the two. The massive stone figure of Vaineteya, or the mythical sun-bird Garuḍa, at Changunarayan, is also an example of early sculpture of the fifth century A.D.

A remarkable limestone statue of a royal personage at Mṛgasthalī, Pashupati, perhaps slightly antedates the above two images of Vishnu Vikranta, i.e. Vishnu in the extended posture. Portrait statues have an important place in Indian art. The grand statue of the Kuṣāṇa Emperor Kaniṣka of the first century A.D. is an outstanding example of Indian sculpture. Indian Kuṣāṇa coins, available in Nepal, also display portraits of kings, but the statue of a king at Mṛgasthalī has Nepali physiognomical features. As pointed out by Dr. Stella Kramrisch, its facial features are mongoloid and more like those of a child but also show the same kind of determination as the kings' faces in pre-Khmer sculpture.[3]

The image of Vishnu in his manifestation as the wild boar at Dhumvarahi is also said to belong to the fifth century A.D. Three other pieces of Vaishnava sculpture of the Licchavi period that deserve mention are the image of Vishnu mounted on Garuḍa, the mythical sunbird, the image of Vishnu mentioned in a Jiṣṇu Gupta inscription of the seventh century and the image of Vishnu lying supine in a pool of water at Budhanilakantha outside Kathmandu.

The Licchavis were themselves followers of Vaishnavism but they did not discourage Buddhism or Shaivism. Remarkable among the masterpieces of Licchavi sculpture of the fifth Century A.D. is an individual image of the Buddha, half-buried in the sands, on the bank of the Bagmati river in the vicinity of the Pashupatinath temple. In the same area, on the left bank of the Bagmati River and half-buried in the ground, is a lovely one-faced (*ekamukha*) Shivalinga. The exquisitely carved face of Shiva resembles the Buddha's face in its infinite serenity and purity.

There is evidence of Nepal's contact with the Indian schools of sculpture in Mathura and Central India during the fifth and sixth centuries. However, we do not know how these contacts came about. Dr. Stella Kramrisch, however, has rightly noted that 'traits of these several Indian schools mingle in Nepal, but whichever components prevail they are subsumed to a whole which is Nepali'.[4]

By the seventh century, the Deccan and Western India had left their permanent mark on Indian tradition in art and sculpture. Nepali sculpture also displays some features of the Aurangabad cave sculpture and the western Indian school of North Gujarat (*samalaji*).

The sculptured figures of 'pilgrims in the mountains' near Kathesimbhu at Kathmandu are of the seventh century A.D. These figures are set against rugged cubist configurations which represent rocks and symbolic nature. This is in keeping with the pattern evolved in India over a millennium from the time of Barhut. Dr. Kramrisch takes special notice of a 'loving presentation of children and flowers' and states that Nepali sculpture has excelled in the creation of images of childhood in many figures of nameless children. The flying celestial beings (*vidyadhara*) in Nepali sculpture are not charismatic youth heroes nor the flying angelic *devatas* of Indian reliefs, but 'children of god' (*devaputra*) who know how to fly.[5] Near the old palace at Kathmandu there is a piece of Nepali sculpture which dates back to the seventh century and shows the subjugation of the serpent Kaliya by Krishna. The godlike Krishna, who subjugates the serpent in this sculpture, is a child and not an adolescent as in Indian sculpture.

Images of the Buddha and the *bodhisattva* Padmapāṇi dating from the seventh century are found at Lagan and at Dhvākā Bāhā in Kathmandu. They are carved between pilasters in niches that face the compass points. These pilasters and niches stand on a pedestal which lends support to the stūpa. In architectural setting, they are related to the Daśāvatāra temple at Deogarh in Uttar Pradesh, India. Although the latter is more detailed and sophisticated than the Nepali specimens mentioned above, the modeling of the images at Dhvākā Bāhā strengthens the purity of the contour through suppression of details. Among the Buddhist religious images of the Licchavi era mention must also be made of the image of Bhagavat Avalokiteśvara at Patan and the small *caityas* or *stūpas* of Chabel among others.

Although the worship of a goddess as Śakti, or the source of power, had not attained the same measure of popularity as it did during the medieval years, statues of goddesses were not unknown during the Licchavi period. Bhagavatī literally means a goddess and implies the female counterpart of Shiva, i.e. Pārvāti in her different manifestations as Dūrgā, Kāli, etc. While nothing definite can be stated about the images of this goddess, known as Dakṣiṇkālī at Pharping, Sobhābhaghavati at Vijeśvari and Bhagavatī at Naxal, there is no doubt that an image of Bhagavatī was set up at Palanchok in the Licchavi period. According to an inscription in the last-named temple, the image was put up by Vijayaswāminī in A.D. 505. It is perhaps the oldest image of a goddess in Nepal and represents the first specimen of the Śaktā cult which later became dominant.

The early part of the seventh century was characterised by great sculptural achievements in Nepal as in India. The masterpieces of this period provided inspiration for Nepali sculptors for the next five hundred years. From the second half of the seventh century onwards, both Hindu and Buddhist cult images became very popular in Nepal. They often consist of three images in which the figure of the main deity, recognised by virtue of its size and central position, dominates the other two minor figures. The figure of Vishnu, accompanied by Lakshmi and Garuḍa in their standing position, is the typical Hindu version. The Buddhist counterpart is the figure of Avalokiteśvara accompanied by two worshipping female guardian deities (*yakṣiṇī*) on their knees. The image of Viṣṇu Śrīdhara of the ninth century at Changunarayan is another example of the Hindu type, while the image of Padmāpaṇi Lokeśvara, dating from the end of the seventh or the early eighth century, near Yampī Bahī in Patan affords an illustration of the Buddhist type. Among the Buddhist cult images dating from before A.D. 800, the image of Padmāpaṇi Lokeśvara at Sigha Bāhā, Kathesimbu in Kathmandu may also be mentioned. The black limestone statue of Maya Devī, Buddha's mother, at Sundhara in Deupatan is more sophisticated than the image of Padmāpaṇi at Sigha Bāhā and is reminiscent of the forms of Gaurī and the Yakṣiṇīs from Mathura.

Vishnu was not the only Hindu god to receive homage from Nepali sculptors, Shiva also came in for his share. There is an array of representations of Umā-Maheśvara depicting the great lord together with his consort Umā and attendants. The image of Umā-Maheśvara at Nagal Tole in Kathmandu belongs to the eighth or ninth century and displays a complex iconography which blends the contemporary Deccan influences, such as those of Ellora, with central and northern Indian motifs. It is interesting to note that the eastern school of Indian art did not contribute anything to this kind of image, despite the fact that this school sent its manuscripts and artists to Nepal from about the year A.D.1000. In the images of the eastern school, Umā sits on the lap of the god, but in the Nepali cult image Shiva embraces with his hand the goddess who sits next to him and rests her hand on his leg. Similarly, in the Umā-Maheśvara bronze of Nepal of the eighth-ninth century, which is kept in the Baroda Museum and picture gallery in India, Umā is not seated on the lap of the god. However, one image of the Shiva family at Patan, which shows Pārvatī seated on the left thigh of Shiva who has his left leg bent as in a posture of sitting cross-legged, is typical of the eastern school of Indian art. Exquisitely wrought and chiselled Shivalingas and Vaishnava pillars with Vishnu seated on his traditional mount Garuḍa, the royal eagle, are frequently encountered and include some outstanding examples of the Licchavi tradition in sculpture.

During the rule of the Pala dynasty (A.D. 750-1150) in eastern India, bronzes made in Nalanda were sent to Nepal where they were re-cast in the Nepali style as is attested by the aforementioned Umā-Maheśvara bronze. In the eleventh century, Nalanda was replaced by Vikramasila as the centre of the Buddhist religion and studies. The Nepali bronzes of this period, in the opinion of Dr. Kramrisch, parallel the phases of Pala sculpture but also tend to borrow from the ornate maturity of the Sena sculpture a delicacy of feeling which is lacking in the East Indian bronzes. The Nepali bronzes, however, excel those of the subsequent Sena dynasty in Eastern India.[6]

Nepali sculpture draws on the resources of India and on its own none-too-well established tradition but seems to gather momentum as it proceeds from one work to another. Dr. Kramrisch has analysed the process in the following terms:

> Confirmed in its own ways, a local tradition tests its strength against the inflowing Indian types. Transplanted into the body of Nepali art, their cumulative combinations and exchanges are part of its substance and are transformed with it, while one or the other motif is carried along as a residual shape in a new context. Eclecticism and conscious borrowing are part of this process. . . . The art of Nepal is not a regional school of Indian art. It is on the receiving end of a one-way traffic. No art forms flow from Nepal to India, they stay in the mountain kingdom having received the impress of their makers, the Newars.[7]

Bronze sculptures and sculptures cast in other metals were also made in the Licchavi period. However specimens from this period have become rare. Some of these rare pieces have been smuggled out of the country. One such sculpture is an image of the Buddha which is inscribed and dated with a date corresponding to A.D. 591.

A lovely copper image of a goddess standing on a lotus pedestal *māhabhujapīṭha*, reproduced in Dr. Stella Kramrisch's book, *The Art of Nepal*, belongs to the seventh century and is a fine specimen of Nepali art in metal statuary.[8] This shows that metal statuary was not merely keeping pace with stone sculpture during the seventh century but actually surpassed it. In this connection, the metal image of the Buddha, discovered for the first time by Dr. Balaram Das, and dated between the fifth and the sixth century A.D., may also be mentioned.

Terracotta was another avenue used by the artists of this time to express their artistic skills. Some specimens of their art have been recovered during trial archaeological excavations done at two sites within the Kathmandu Valley.

Literature

Sanskrit was the court and literary language of Nepal during the Licchavi period. It was used in inscriptions and royal edicts of the time. The quality and standard of the Sanskrit verse inscribed on the stone-slabs are proof of the literary and intellectual achievement of the Licchavis, which equalled the aesthetic success in the field of architecture and sculpture. The Licchavi period has accurately been described by historians as the 'Golden Age' of Nepali history.

Nepal, along with India, made contributions to the renaissance in Tibet both in the time of the Licchavi King Narendradeva and subsequently. Tibetan kings and abbots employed Nepali teachers of Buddhism to copy Buddhist religious manuscripts and also to translate them into Tibetan from Sanskrit. Nepali artists and architects were hired to build the stupas and monasteries and to decorate them with paintings and murals. Teachers like Śīla Mañjuśrī and Buddhakīrti, of the Licchavi era, rendered as much service to the cause of religious reform and revival in Tibet as did Śāntarakṣita, Padmasaṃbhava and Atīśa of the early medieval period.

NOTES

1. The best explanation in English of the Lichhavi administrative, land and taxation terms is contained in Prayag Raj Sharma, 'The Land System of the Licchavis in Nepal', *Kailash* (1983) X, 1-2:11-62.
2. *Ibid.* p. 38.

3. Stella Kramrisch, *The Art of Nepal*, Philadelphia Asia House Gallery, 1964, p. 23.
4. *Ibid.*
5. *Ibid.*, p. 24.
6. *Ibid.*, p. 40.
7. *Ibid.*, p. 48.
8. *Ibid.*

CHAPTER IV

THE DAWN OF THE MEDIEVAL ERA (A.D. 880-1200)

In view of the confusion about the so-called Thakuri dynasty in the ancient and medieval history of Nepal, a few words about it may not be out of place here. In the works on the history of Nepal, the term '*ṭhakurī*' is applied to three sets of rulers during the Licchavi period and the following periods: The first set of rulers from Aṃśuvarman (A.D. 605-1043), the Thakuris of Nuwakot (c. A.D. 1043-1082), and the Thakuris of Patan (c. A.D. 1082-1200). Since the Thakuris of Patan and those of Nuwakot overlap and alternate on the throne, the above classification is not of much service.

Moreover, in view of the fact that the Licchavis were of the Sun Dynasty (*sūryavaṃśī*), the pre-Malla rulers, from A.D. 879 through 1200, who are said to have belonged to the Thakuri dynasty, may as well be regarded as the later Licchavis. The term 'Thakuri' does not occur in the earlier chronicles which use the word '*sūryavaṃśī*''. But the epithet '*sūryavaṃśī*' would apply to the Mallas also, as they too claimed solar descent. However, the later Nepali chronicles of the eighteenth and nineteenth centuries used the term 'Thakuri' to distinguish the predecessors of the Mallas from both the Licchavis and the Mallas. By the eighteenth and nineteenth centuries, there had arisen a general impression that rulers everywhere in Nepal as well as in India were Thakuris or Thakurs. In fact the term has long been used in the hills to denote anyone who claimed Rajput descent. Hence to call the kings between the Licchavi and Malla periods 'Thakuri' and to refer to the period as the 'Thakuri Period' is neither very accurate nor informative. Mary Slusser in her work on the cultural history of the Valley has called the period 'The Transitional Period'[1] and Petech in his revised edition has adopted the same term.[2] However, a transitional period of over 300 years sounds strange indeed and would seem to indicate a transition from one clear-cut situation to another which is not at all the case.

The early medieval history of Nepal is full of confusion. The duplication of names within the same chronicle, together with the divergence of names and their order in different chronicles makes the confusion worse. There are different versions of the names of the successors of the Licchavis or the later Licchavis. For example, the *Gopālarājavaṃśāvalī* and the chronicle used by Kirkpatrick, mention Rāghavadeva, who is said to have founded the Newari or Nepal Era (Nepāl Saṃvat) on 20 October 879 A.D. The era did indeed begin on this date, but the name of this king does not occur in the genealogical lists given in the chronicles used by Daniel Wright, Bhagavanlal Indraji, Sylvain Levi, and Cecil Bendall. It does not occur in the later Sanskrit chronicles nor in the Nepali chronicles which have been more recently published.

We have only two historical documents, both confirming the reign of Saṅkaradeva I, for the first few kings of this period. The most reliable chronicles the *Gopālarājavaṃśāvalī* and the chronicle used by Kirkpatrick give different lists, but the above two documents have shown that the one used by Kirkpatrick is the correct one. The first king was Rāghavadeva who founded the new era in A.D. 879. He was followed by Śaṅkaradeva who was ruling in A.D. 920. He was in turn followed by Sahadeva and Vikramadeva. After Vikramadeva the order of succession is clear from contemporary documents, i.e. manuscript colophons and inscriptions.[3]

The next king is Guṇakāmadeva I who ruled from about A.D. 980 to 998. Both the *Gopālarājavaṃśāvali* and the chronicle used by Kirkpatrick give this king an impossibly long reign of 85 years and 6 months. He certainly was no longer ruling by the end of the year 998 and his reign cannot have started much earlier than 980. The long reign perhaps relates to the very high profile he has in Nepal's history of this period; he is a dominant figure in a line of shadowy and insignificant kings. According to the later chronicles he founded the city of Kathmandu[4] and made lavish donations to the temple of Pashupatinath. In the oral tradition almost anything really old is ascribed to Guṇakāmadeva.

A manuscript colophon of the year A.D. 889-90 notes that in that year Guṇakāmadeva 'established his sole rule'.[5] This implies that up to this point he shared the rule with someone else. This points to a phenomenon which occurs repeatedly in this period known as *dvairājya* (or *dvirajyāka* in the Nepali documents), some sort of joint rule. Two types of joint rule are known in Sanskrit literature. It could mean the joint rule of two kings, of equal rank, each ruling over one half of a kingdom which was still considered to be one kingdom. In this case one half of the kingdom could in turn be ruled jointly by two kings. The other type of joint rule consisted of co-rulership by two kings on the throne without involving a partition of the kingdom. This type is clearly attested to in some of the situations of this period where we find the term *ubhayarājya* 'joint-rule'. Though Guṇakāmadeva put an end to this double rule, it was revived after his death by Narendradeva I (c. A.D. 998-999) and Udayadeva (c.998-1004), in this case a true joint-rule (*ubhayarajya*). These two are followed by three overlapping kings: Nirbhayadeva (c. 1004-1009), Rudradeva I (c. 1007-1028) and Bhojadeva (c.1009-1020). There are seven documents from this period which sketch a very complicated situation. Petech speculates that this is what happened:

> Nirbhayadeva succeeded Udayadeva. In 1005 he was alone on the throne; then about 1008 he took as colleague Rudradeva I. Nirbhayadeva died a few years later. Rudradeva's grand-nephew Bhojadeva proclaimed himself king at Kathmandu at some time before 1011; but in 1012 and 1015 he recognized again Rudradeva as his senior partner. Both reigned at Patan, while in 1015 Lakṣmīkāmadeva ruled the other half of the Kingdom (perhaps from Kathmandu). Then Bhojadeva disappeared, and in 1028 Rudradeva was reigning alone in his share of the kingdom, which after his death was taken over by Lakṣmīkāmadeva.[6]

Lakṣmīkāmadeva ruled from about A.D. 1010 to 1041. The *Gopālarāja-vaṃśāvalī* credits Lakṣmīkāmadeva with bringing peace to the country after a struggle. This may refer to a unification of the two half kingdoms. However, peace did not last. A manuscript copied in A.D.1039 refers to a great war raging in Bhaktapur.[7]

The chronicles refer to the next king by different names: Vijayadeva, Jayadeva and Jayakāmadeva. We have no contemporary documents referring to his rule but he must have ruled from about A.D. 1030 until 1037. Petech speculates that perhaps he was a sort of junior king under Lakṣmīkāmadeva who eventually deposed him. Later after the civil war of 1039 referred to above, he reappears in collaboration with Lakṣmīkāmadeva I's successor Bhāskaradeva (c. 1039-1048).

Bhāskaradeva seems to have been the sole ruler for the last few years of his reign, but his reign was followed by the joint rule of

Baladeva (c. 1048-1060) and Yiśadeva (c. 1048-1049). Yiśadeva's role in this partnership was short-lived and for most of his reign Bhāskaradeva ruled alone. This reign also seems to have been the last example of joint or divided rule.

Bhāskaradeva was succeeded by Pradymnakāmadeva (c.1060-1066) and Nāgārjunadeva (c.1066-1069). Next came Śaṅkaradeva II (c.1069-1082) who seems to have been a ruler of some stature. The *Gopālarājavaṃśāvalī* credits him with making an image of Śaṅkesvara at Naxal and completing a temple there. Above all, he kept the country at peace. But the peace was short-lived. According to the chronicles Śaṅkaradeva II was expelled by Vāmadeva (1082-1085), a descendant of Aṃśuvarman through a side-line who became king with the help of the Thakuris of Thankot, Patan and Kathmandu. Harṣadeva (c. 1085-1098) succeeded Vāmadeva. Harṣadeva was a weak king and his reign ushered in a period of disorder and instability.

Entry of Nānyadeva into Nepal's History

Towards the end of the eleventh century, a new ruler came into power and prominence in Tirhut, which adjoins Nepal's boundary in the south. His name was Nānyadeva. Nanyadeva's family were originally from Karnataka like the family of Vijaya Sena, Nānyadeva's contemporary and founder of the Sena dynasty in Bengal. The emergence of southern rulers in northern India is attributed to the military expeditions of the Chalukya Kings Someśvara I and Vikramāditya VI. At the beginning of his career Nānyadeva was merely a local feudal chief (*māhasāmantādhipati*). In A.D. 1097 he proclaimed himself king and founded a new capital at Simraungarh (in the present Nepal tarai). At some date, that is now unknown, he invaded Nepal.

The later Nepal chronicles refer to him as a prince of Karnataka who came to north in A.D. 889 [sic], entered Nepal, conquered it, dethroning two of the Malla kings whom he forced to flee to the plains, and established his court at Bhaktapur. This whole account is, as Professor Petech says, 'a tissue of chronological absurdities (including the names of non-existing kings)'[8] which was first fabricated by the late Malla kings to claim descent from Nānyadeva. However, it led many astray. Levi believed in Nānyadeva's conquest of Nepal on the authority of these late chronicles. Indian historians of repute, such as Dr. R.C. Majumdar and Dr. H.C. Ray Chaudhury took their cue from Levi.

The rulers of Simraungarh are referred to in the *Gopālarājavaṃśāvali* under the name of the Doya, i.e. the people of Tirhut. The first reference to them is under the date of 27th August 1111 when one Śrī Naramalladeva cut to pieces the Doya. Naramalladeva must have been a local chieftain, but what is clear from the reference is that Nānyadeva did raid Nepal and may have even entered the Valley but was defeated and driven back to Tirhut. Further raids are referred to in the time of the Malla kings, but the Ḍoya never conquered the Valley.

The arguments against Nānyadeva's conquest of Nepal may be briefly summed up as follows: The Nepali kings are found ruling undisturbed at the time when they are supposed to have been under attack from Nānyadeva; genealogical and chronological difficulties arise if one accepts Nānyadeva as the founder of a new dynasty in Nepal; there is a dearth of contemporary evidence to support these claims.[9]

To return to our narrative, the anarchy which followed Harṣadeva's reign resulted in the temporary rise of independent feudatories. These included Rāmadeva of Dhavalaśrotrī of mid-Western Nepal. Rāmadeva seems to have claimed absolute independence but soon had to retreat from this position.

The period of chaos and uncertainty came to an end with the revival of the old dynasty by Śivadeva (1098-1126). He was the son of the Śaṇkaradeva who was expelled by Vāmadeva and had ruled before Harṣadeva. Śivadeva made donations to Pashupati and built a palace at Kirti-Bhaktapur, i.e. modern Kirtipur. He struck both gold and silver coins and forced the feudatory Rāmadeva to recognise his suzerainty over Dhavalaśrotrī in the Magar area.

At this point a serious problem of chronology arises. There are six documents from A.D. 1105 to 1122 which attest to a king called Siṃhadeva. These documents are completely included within the reign of Śivadeva. Do we have here a king with two names or a return of the old joint rule? A definite answer cannot be given to this question, but after considering all the evidence and the arguments pro and con, both Petech and the Nepali historian Dhanavajra Vajracarya plead for Śivadeva and Siṃhadeva being one and the same man.[10]

Śivadeva's immediate successor was Indradeva (c.1126-1136) who was supported by the Jīva chiefs of Udayapur. The Jīvas of Udayapur must have attained prominence during the period of chaos. Even after the restoration of the dynastic rulers, the Jīva chiefs continued as powers behind the throne. It seems that they supported Vāmadeva and Siṃhadeva (= Śivadeva?), but at this point abandoned the descendants of Siṃhadeva. Siṃhadeva's rightful heir, Mahendradeva, never ruled but was passed over in favour of an elder half brother. After Indradeva we hear no more of the Jīva chiefs.

Indradeva was followed by Mānadeva (c. 1136-1140), Narendradeva II (1140-1147), and Ānandadeva (1147-1167). Ānandadeva's coronation marked the return of Siṃhadeva's direct line. The chronicle speaks in glowing terms of this king who is credited with a number of foundations, the most important of which may be his building of a royal palace in Bhaktapur known as the Tipura (or Tripura) Palace.[11] His was a long, peaceful and prosperous reign but turmoil and disunity were just over the horizon.

Ānandadeva was succeeded by Rudradeva II (1167-1175) and Amṛtadeva (1176-1178). Amṛtadeva's reign was marked by a disastrous famine as a result of which the price of grain rose and food became scarce. He was succeeded by Someśvaradeva (1178-1183/5), the son of the prince Mahendradeva (son of Siṃhadeva) who never ruled. In 1184, a new king, called Guṇakāmadeva II appeared upon the scene. He ruled for at least three years. Guṇakāmadeva II is followed by two overlapping kings: Lakṣmīkāmadeva II (c. 1192-1197) and Vijayakāmadeva (c. 1192-1200) who may well have been sons or at least relatives of Guṇakāmadeva. It was a time of confusion and civil strife. Nothing is known about the relationship between these two kings except that from about 1192 to 1197 Kathmandu was definitely included in the dominion of Lakṣmīkāmadeva II. On this note of confusion the period of the successors of the Licchavi and the so-called Thakuri dynasties comes to an end.

NOTES

1. Mary S. Slusser, *Nepal Mandala: A Cultural Study of the Kathmandu Valley*, Princeton, Princeton University Press, 1982, p. 41 ff.
2. Luciano Petech *Medieval History of Nepal*, Second Edition, Roma, Instituto Italiano per il Medio ed Estreno Oriente, 1984, p. 31 ff. Petech's first edition (1958) was a pioneering work on this period. Since that time considerable primary research has been done on the period by a variety of Nepalese scholars and published in Nepali in a number of different periodicals. Both Petech in his second edition and Slusser in her book have made full use of this new material, and hence both have made a significant contribution to Nepalese history by collecting and integrating this new material into a single volume in English and making it available to a larger public.
3. Petech, p. 32.
4. Deviprasda Lamsal, ed., *Bhāṣā Vaṃśāvalī*, Part II. Kathmandu, National Library, p. 23.
5. Petech, p. 33
6. *Ibid.*, p. 37
7. *Ibid.*, p. 39.
8. *Ibid.*, p. 55.

9. The first evidence of this fabrication appears to be an inscription of King Pratapa Malla of Kathmandu.
10. Petech, pp. 53-4; Dhanavarajya Vajracarya 'Madhyākalik Nepālkā ek Prakhyāt RājāSivadeva', *Contributions to Nepalese Studies*, 8, 1 (1980) 207-222.
11. It has been maintained that from time of the founding of this palace Bhadgaun became the Capital city of Nepal and that there is little or no evidence that Patan was ever the Capital (Slusser, p. 123). Not all writers have accepted this theory, including Petech (see p. 188). What is clear is that from this time forward the kings had a residence in Bhadgaun and one in Patan. Which was the major residence, or the *de facto* capital, is still a matter of discussion; but it is clear that at least from the time of the third Malla king Jayadeva [A.D. 1255-1258]) the political activity was centred in Bhadgaun.

CHAPTER V

THE EARLY MALLAS

The Mallas, like the Licchavis, appear and reappear on the scene of Indian history. The word '*malla*' in Sanskrit means a wrestler and is sometimes adopted by rulers, like the Pallavas of Kanchi in India, as a title to signify their skill or success in wrestling contests with their adversaries and rivals. Early Buddhist texts mention a republican confederation of the Mallas whose territory adjoined that of the Licchavis. Kushinagara and Pava were known as Mallapuri, or the cities of the Mallas. Despite the attempt of the later Nepali chronicles to link the Nepali Mallas with Nānyadeva and Harisiṃhadeva of Tirhut, the ancestry of the Malla rulers in the Kathmandu Valley is obscure.

Ari Malla (A.D.1200-1216), the son of one Jayasi Malla, was the first Malla king of the Kathmandu Valley. We do not know how he acquired the throne, whether by conquest, election or dynastic link. The last known document of the Thakuri King Vijayakāmadeva, the last ruler of the earlier dynasty is dated January 1200, and the first colophon of Ari Malla's reign is dated October 1200 (or possibly 1199). It may, therefore, be correct to assume that the Malla dynasty was established in A.D.1200. Ari Malla's titles in the successive colophons reveal the gradual consolidation of his authority. The earlier documents of his reign refer to him merely as *rājā* or *nṛpa*, whereas only in 1211 is he given the full royal title: *rājādhirāja parameśvara paramabhaṭṭāraka.*

His son and successor, Abhaya Malla (1216-1255), had acquired considerable learning before he became king. His reign was turbulent because he was at first challenged by one Raṇaśūra, who may have been a claimant to the Nepali throne or one of the lesser kings of the western hills. On 24th May 1244 the Ḍoya (the Tirhutiyas from Simraungarh) invaded Nepal through the Khandadhara forest but were driven off with heavy losses by the Commander in Chief, Anarghamalladeva, evidently a member of the royal family. Later the same year, another raid, perhaps again by the Ḍoyas, was repulsed by one Amaru Mahātha who set out from Palanchok. He routed the invaders and returned in a triumphant procession. In 1245 the Ḍoya returned again and advanced as far as Gokarna where they were defeated. In the course of a number of petty skirmishes within the kingdom, one Jayaśiha Malla (or Jayasiṃha Malla), based in Bhadgaun and the son of one Jagataneka Malla, emerges as a power to be reckoned with. Abhaya Malla's reign, which also had its share of famine, plague and serious earthquakes, was not a prosperous one. A disastrous earthquake occurred on 7th June 1255. One-third of the population perished and the king himself was seriously injured dying of his injuries six days later.

Abhaya Malla was succeeded by his son Jayadeva Malla (1255-1258) whose reign also suffered a series of natural calamities—earthquakes and famine. The monarchy itself was weakened by a struggle between the Jayaśiha Malla mentioned above and one Jayabhīmadeva. Jayabhīmadeva was the feudal lord of Bhonta, the region of Banepa east of the Kathmandu Valley. Jayaśiha Malla was building his own extensive following within the city of Bhadgaun. His descendants are referred to as the Tripura royal family (*rājakula*) after the royal palace in Bhadgaun where they lived. The rest of this period is marred by the struggle between the house of Bhonta and the house of Tripura. The situation was complicated by the fact that the royal family was dying out. Jayadeva had two sons both of whom died in childhood. Jayadeva's reign was marked by a number of revolts and clashes between the contending forces within the Valley. Jayaśiha Malla and Jayabhīmadeva were the principal contenders with Jayabhīmadeva often siding with the reigning monarch. Jayadeva died on 19th March 1258 and two months later Jayabhīmadeva and Jayaśiha Malla were encamped near Palanchok which they had jointly subdued. Out of this association came an agreement between the two rivals that henceforth the two houses of Bhonta and Tripura would share the throne alternately. Though there is no documentary proof of this agreement, this is in fact what happened more or less regularly over the next one hundred years.

From this point on to the time of Jayasthiti Malla the later chronicles do not correspond at all to the older ones such as the *Gopālarāja-vaṃśāvalī*, the chronicle used by Kirkpatrick and the so-called 'Kaiser Vaṃśāvalī'. It is at this point that the later chronicles bring in the list of the Tirhutiya kings, allegedly descended from the line of Nānyadeva and Harisiṃhadeva , neither of whom reigned in the Valley. This is a result of a deliberate falsification of history perpetrated by the descendants of Jayasthiti Malla. This falsification first appears in a seventeenth century inscription of Pratāpa Malla and was taken up by the later writers and incorporated into the later chronicles.

After the agreement cited above, Jayabhīmadeva became king and ruled until 1271 when he was succeeded by Jayaśiha Malla who ruled until 1274. Thus the kingship shifted again from the house of Bhonta to the house of Tripura. Jayabhīmadeva is never referred to as 'Malla' and Jayaśiha Malla, who was the son of one Jagataneka Malla, may or may not have been a relation of the Malla royal family. Hence we are dealing with two new dynasties alternating on the throne. Jayaśiha Malla had a short reign when he either abdicated or was deposed in 1274 or 1275 to be followed by Ananta Malla (c. 1274-1308). Jayaśiha Malla died only in A.D.1287.

Ananta Malla, whose ancestry is not known, reigned for 34 years and during this time dealt with the Mongol Court in China, not directly, but through the Sakya Monastery in Tibet which enjoyed the favour of the Emperor Kublai Khan. Kublai Khan ordered the erection of a golden stupa in Tibet for his teacher Sa-skya-pa Lama, and, by 1260, during the rule of Jayabhīmadeva, Nepali artisans were sent to undertake the task. In response to a request from the Sa-skya-pa Lama a group of Nepali artisans, under the leadership of A-ni-ko (A.D.1245-1306) was sent to Lhasa. Although A-ni-ko is not mentioned in the Nepali chronicles, information available in the Chinese annals reveals that close relations existed between Nepal and the great monasteries of central Tibet. According to the Chinese account A-ni-ko was a descendant of the royal family of Nepal.

During the last thirteen years of Ananta Malla's reign Nepal was invaded both from the west and the south. In the winter of 1287-1288 Jitāri (or Jayatāri) Malla of the other Malla dynasty from the Khasa area in the Karnali region, invaded the Kathmandu Valley. According to the chronicles the city dwellers sought shelter in the neighbouring forests, but returned when the invaders left. Jitāri Malla came again in March of 1289. This time he burned down several villages but paid visits to Swayambhu and Bungadya (Matsyendranath) and then made religious offerings to Pashupatinath before leaving. In February of 1290 he returned once again taking Nuwakot on his way. He again visited Matsyendranath and Pashupatinath. After this he put some villages to the torch and then spent one month at a fort in Patan which he destroyed before leaving.

In December of 1291 the Ḍoya from Tirhut again attacked Nepal from the south penetrating as far as Bhadgaun. The same invaders reappeared in 1300 and, after taking several places which can no longer be identified, they attacked Bhadgaun. They inflicted a fine on the house of Tripura and levies were laid on the populace to buy off the Ḍoya. Eventually they were satisfied and in March they withdrew. There is evidence that the Ḍoya were actually called by the reigning monarch and the house of Bhonta to put an end to the claims of the house of Tripura. After their withdrawal the kingdom was once again wrecked by internal strife resulting from the rivalry between these two factions. Sick of the constant bickering and fighting, Ananta Malla took all his treasure and the treasure of the Bhadgaun temples and donated this to Pashupatinath in 1307. He then withdrew to Bhonta though he continued to be recognised as the king until he died in August of 1308 at Banepa.

During this period the house of Tripura was out of power and the house of Bhonta under the leadership of Jayādityadeva, the elder son of King Jayabhīmadeva was the power behind the throne. It was most probably Jayāditya who had arranged the abdication of Jayaśiha Malla and he who put in Ananta Malla as a puppet ruler. Jayādityadeva was made heir apparent and soon came into conflict with his younger half-brother Jayānandadeva whom he then imprisoned at Palanchok. Jayāditya died in 1292 and his widow, Vīramadevi filled in his position until her son Jayaśaktideva could come of age.

With the death of Ananta Malla the struggle between the two houses broke out again. The house of Tripura, under Jayatuṅga Malla, son of Jayaśiha Malla, took several places to the west of the Valley and at one point Banepa itself was conquered. Jayaśaktideva was too weak to press his claim to the vacant throne, and his despondency led him to a fatal mistake: he called on the Ḍoya for help. In March of 1311 the Ḍoya came, occupied a part of the city of Patan, destroyed religious objects, imprisoned the Brahmans and all the local noblemen and destroyed the palace. After this they exacted war expenses from the local people and set several buildings on fire. But then Jayaśaktideva had trouble getting rid of his saviours. They began to loot the treasury in Deopatan and later set off towards Sanga. Several people from Banepa were killed. Finally in March of 1312 the Ḍoya withdrew and started off for home. Though the Nepali chronicles do not mention the name of the Ḍoya commander at this time, Mithila sources claim that one Candeśvara, a minister of King Harasiṃha of Tirhut conquered Nepal at this time, vanquished the ruler of Nepal and touched the image of Pashupati. This exaggerated claim probably refers to the one year occupation of Patan by the Ḍoya who were invited by Jayaśaktideva.

The year 1312 saw the arrival of another force. The Khasya king Ripu Malla, after visiting Lumbini—where he and his son immortalised themselves by scratching their names on the Ashokan pillar—entered Nepal. He took a ceremonial bath at the Bungamati shrine of Matsyendranath and worshipped both at the Pashupatinath shrine and Swayambhu. Eighteen days later he departed. This was not an invasion or even a raid but more in the nature of a religious pilgrimage. However, it has been suggested that he came at the behest of the Tripura faction to counter the occupation of the Ḍoya.[1] Perhaps—but he was a year too late.

This struggle between the two houses resulted in the complete collapse of the power and prestige of the monarchy and untold suffering for the people. The agreement between the two houses had broken down and local feudatories began to enjoy a greater measure of autonomy, the most well known of which were the ruler of Pharping and the chief of Nuwakot. Jayaśaktideva, perhaps discredited by his shameful role in the whole affair, disappears from the chronicles. Jayatuṅga Malla of Tripura died in 1312. His young son, Jayarudra Malla (born 1295), became the heir of the Tripura fortunes.

The *Gopālarājavaṃśāvalī* notes that in November of 1311 an expedition set off from Banepa towards Tripura and the people of Bhadgaun fled. This took place, it says, during the reign of Jayarudra Malla and his mother Padumalladevī.[2] It is difficult to evaluate this entry, but it seems that at this time Jayarudra Malla was recognised as the *de facto* ruler of Bhadgaun. In 1313, after the retreat of the Ḍoya, Jayarudra Malla went to Patan to attend the Matsyendranath festival. He stayed for ten days and put to death five of the leading noblemen. This seems to indicate that he took charge of Patan and eliminated the heads of the opposition. From this point on the house of Tripura had the upper hand, and Jayarudra Malla and his mother were the wielders of real power behind the throne.

By 1313 Nepal had been five years without a recognised king and it was time to rectify the situation. Rather than try to claim the throne himself Jayarudra Malla made peace with the house of Bhonta by putting a Bhonta ruler on the throne. However, he chose not Śaktideva but Śaktideva's aged uncle Jayānandadeva who had once been imprisoned by his brother Jayādityadeva. Though he was universally recognised as the legitimate monarch by all, Jayānandadeva continued to reside in Palanchok. In the meantime Jayarudra Malla continued to attack various places around the Valley and bring them under his power. By 1320 he withdrew his support for Jayānandadeva and crowned Jayāri Malla, his relative, as king. Jayāri Malla, who ruled until 1344, was the son of Ananta Malla, and his power was more apparent than real, like that of his father. Jayarudra Malla continued to exercise real power, though without any title.

During this period Harisiṃhadeva, the ruler of Tirhut fled his capital of Simraungarh in A.D.1324-25 when his kingdom was annexed by Ghiyas ud-din Tughlaq, the king of Delhi. Sylvain Levi and other writers, misinterpreting an old Sanskrit verse, had assumed Harisiṃhadeva invaded Nepal. Actually, Harisiṃhadeva never went back to Tirhut where the Sultan set up a vassal state under Kāmeśvara, the founder of the Oniwāra dynasty. Harisiṃhadeva and his court fled to the hills of the Dholakha area where he died at a place called Timpata in 1326. His son and ministers were arrested by a local chieftain and their wealth seized. Another contemporary account notes that his wife Devalakṣmīdevī and his son with their relatives entered Nepal as refugees.[3] It is known from later events that the members of this court were received as honoured guests by Jayarudra Malla's family and exercised a considerable influence over events in the succeeding decades. A recently published chronicle, which appears to be a complete version of the truncated 'Kaiser Vaṃśāvalī', gives the reason for this royal reception: Devaladevī was the daughter of Jayatuṅga Malla and Padumalladevī and hence the sister of Jayarudra Malla.[4]

In June of 1326 the king maker of Bhadgaun, Jayarudra Malla, still a young man of thirty, died. Since he had no male heirs, his daughter Nāyakadevi assumed leadership of the Tripura house, tutored by her grandmother Padumalladevī. For the next two generations the women of the house of Tripura--Padumalladevī, Devaladevī, Nāyakadevī and her daughter played centre stage in the political drama that was acted out in Bhadgaun.

In 1328 the Kathmandu Valley was invaded by another Malla ruler from the Khasa kingdom. The new invader, Āditya Malla, came to Nepal by way of Nuwakot and conquered Pharping. Next he attacked the fort of Patan for twenty-two days but was not able to take it. A Khasya ruler returned one last time in 1334 when the chronicle notes that in September of that year a local feudatory who had entered Patan and tried to exact tribute from the people was killed by the Khasa. Forty men were killed. In turn the Khaṣya ruler exacted a tribute from the people and withdrew only in March of the following year when he had collected his tax. In the meantime he and his followers had burned the town of Sankhu. The name of the Khasa ruler is not mentioned, but Punya Malla was the Khasya ruler from 1336 to 1339. This five-month occupation of Patan was the last incursion of the Khasya rulers into the Valley.

Back in Bhadgaun, Nāyakadevī grew up under the care of her grandmother Padumalladevī. She was married to one Hariścandra who, along with his brother Gopālacandra (or Gopāladeva) were refugees from Kasi. The prince consort was soon caught up in the family struggles and was resented by the local aristocracy. In September of 1332 Padumalladevī died and Hariścandra found it difficult to maintain his place in the old palace of Jayarudra Malla. Finally in May of 1335 he was poisoned by the nobles who boasted of it afterwards. This left Nāyakadevī under the guardianship of her brother-in-law Gopāladeva. Eventually she became the lover of a prince of Tirhut, one Jagatasiṃha. This led to a conflict between Jagatasiṃha and Gopāladeva which ended when Gopāladeva was seized and decapitated by the followers of Jagatasiṃha.

Who was Jagatasiṃha? This is a question which vexed students of this period for a long time. It is clear that he was a Tirhutia prince; most probably he was the son of Harisiṃhadeva. This theory was first put forward by the Nepali historians Dhanavajra Vajracarya and Tulsi Ram Vaidya and has been accepted by Petech in his latest edition.[5] If this is true then it is clear that Devaladevī was indeed the widow of Harisiṃhadeva as confirmed by the independent source which gives Harisiṃhadeva's wife's name as Devalakṣmīdevī. Here is the connection between the late Malla kings and the dynasty of Nānyadeva which Pratāpa Malla and his successors tried to sanitize by falsifying the records to show a direct descent in the male line from Nānyadeva .

Jagatasiṃha seems to have succeeded in reaffirming the ascendancy of the Tripura house but had to contend with the old enemies of the court who made a compact with a shadowy figure called Paṣupati Malla. In January of 1347 a daughter was born to Jagataṣiṃha and Nāyakadevī. She was named Rājalladevī. Ten days later her mother died and about this time Jagatasiṃha himself was thrown into prison and disappeared from the scene. The infant princess was left to the care of old Devaladevī who proved to be an able regent of the fortunes of the Tripura house. In 1348 she was able to have Paṣupati Malla arrested and imprisoned, thus ending the one current threat to the family's fortunes.

Jayāri Malla, the puppet of the house of Tripura had died in 1344. For three years there was no king, for Jayāri Malla had died without an heir and the house of Tripura was going through a difficult period in those days of the rise of Jagatasiṃha. In 1347 Devaladevī reaffirmed her power and made an agreement with the Bhonta house allowing them to supply the reigning monarch while she retained *de facto* control of the Valley. Thus in July of 1347, with the agreement of all parties,

Jayarājadeva of the Bhonta house was crowned king of Nepal at Deopatan and ruled until 1361. Jayarājadeva was the illegitimate son of Jayānandadeva of Bhonta and was born at Palanchok. In the year 1323, when he was only six years old, we hear of him accompanying Jyotirāma Varddhana Mahāta on a journey to Pharping, Patan and Tripura. Jyotirāma Varddhana was from a *vaisya* family of nobles from Banepa who came to play a very large role in the politics of the next two generations. Throughout Jayarājadeva's reign Jyotirāma's son, Anekarāma Varddhana, held the position of prime minister and his son, Jayasiṃharāma Varddhana, was the attendant to the heir apparent, Jayārjunadeva. Devaladevī remained in close contact with these powerful figures and acted in concert with them at critical times. Acting as Regent, Devaladevī played a prominent role in piloting the principality of Bhadgaun through the storm that was about to break over the Valley.

Shumshud-din Iliyas, formerly a vassal of Mahummad Tughlaq, declared himself independent of his overlord and in 1345-46 conquered Tirhut, which the Tughlaq Sultan had settled on Kameśvara of the Oniwāra family, about eleven years earlier. From Tirhut, Iliyas invaded Nepal in 1349 through Janakpur, Sindhuli and Banepa. The Muslim invaders despoiled the temples of their ancient treasure, accumulated from time immemorial, and also destroyed images of gods and goddesses. Although the Muslim invasion had left its visible mark on the Valley, in the shape of damaged and broken images, the myth of Nepal having been unsullied by the taint of Muslim invasion persisted for a long time. It was Dr. K.P. Jayasawal who pointed out the facts of the Muslim invasion, on the basis of the Swayambhu inscription, in an article in the *Journal of the Bihar Research Society* (XXII) in 1936. Dr. R.K. Choudhary reconstructed the background of the events in his article called 'The Oniwāra of Mithila'. It was found later that Jayasawal had slightly misinterpreted the date of invasion as 1346, whereas, in fact, the Swayambhu inscription gives the date as 20 November 1349. This date is also corroborated by the Pim Bahal inscription at Patan and by the *Gopālarājavaṃśāvalī*.

After Shamsud-din Iliyas left Nepal, Devaladevī continued to exert her influence, and in one manuscript colophon of 1353 she is given royal titles and said to be ruling (*vijayarājye*).[6] Whatever the meaning of this stray reference, it is clear that she was in control. In 1354 she arranged the marriage of her grand-daughter and ward, Rājalladevī to one Sthitirāja (or Jayasthiti) Malla.[7] This marriage proved to be an event of great consequence for this man influenced the political destiny of Nepal for the next four centuries. We leave consideration of the last king of this period for the next chapter. His fortunes are entirely enmeshed in the story of the rise of Sthitirāja Malla.

Thus the state of strife and uncertainty that had characterised Ananta Malla's reign continued for another 75 years. The throne was fought over by two factions. The feudal nobles and hill-chiefs became restive and more influential. External invasions by the Ḍoya, the Khasya Malla Kings, and the Muslim ruler of Bengal, aggravated the situation all the more. These chaotic conditions lasted until the throne passed into the hands of Sthitirāja Malla, husband of a distant relative of Ananta Mallas' family on the maternal side. He, at last, succeeded in restoring peace and harmony in strife-torn Nepal.

NOTES

1. See Dhanavajra Vajracarya and Tek Bahadur. Shreshta, Nuvākoṭko *Aitihāsik Rūprekhā* (Kathmandu, 2032 V.S.) 32-33.
2. Dhanavajra Vajracarya and Kamal P. Malla, eds., *The Gopālarājāvaṃśāvalī*, Weisbaden, Franz Steiner Verlag, 1985, 43 kha.
3. See Mohan P. Khanal, 'Itihās Saṃśodhanko Kehī Saṃśodhan', *Ancient Nepal* 3 (October 1970), 46.
4. Kamal P. Malla, 'Nepālavaṃśāvalī: A Complete Version of the Kaiser Vaṃśāvalī', *Contributions to Nepalese Studies* XII, 2 (April 1985) pp. 74-101. This is the only reference to Devaladevī being the daughter of Jayatuṅga Malla and one can certainly question this sole reference. If one accepts it, of course, it raises further serious difficulties: Rajalladevī and Jagatasiṃha were then first cousins. Their cohabitation would certainly have been considered incestuous by Hindu law. On the other hand, the contemporary records make it abundantly clear that they were never married in any formal way and that shortly after the birth of Rajalladevī Jagatasiṃha was thrown into prison. Was this purely a political move or does it indicate the court's disapproval of this highly irregular liaison? The fact that the daughter was accepted as the heir of the fortunes of the house of Jayarudra Malla and played such a prominent role in her lifetime can easily be explained by the force of circumstances: there were no other living heirs.
5. Luciano Petech, *Medieval History of Nepal*, Second Edition, Roma, Instituto Italiano per il Medio ed Estremo Oriente, 1984, p. 120.
6. *Gopalarājāvaṃśāvalī*, 54 ka.
7. Jayasthiti Malla has become the accepted form of this man's name in books on the history of Nepal in English and in many in Nepali, probably because this form of his name appears in the later Nepalese chronicles. However, in contemporary references he is consistently referred to as Sthitarāja or Jayasthitirāja Malla.

CHAPTER VI

JAYASTHITI MALLA AND HIS SUCCESSORS

Some time after his marriage to Rājalladevī, Jayasthiti Malla developed into the key figure in the history and politics of the period. However, because his father was an obscure person, named Aśoka Malla, the later chronicles present him as a descendant of Harisiṃhadeva, which is patently absurd. One chronicle connects him with Nāga Malla, a son of Jayadeva (1255-58), the third of the Malla rulers, in an attempt to make him appear to be a scion of the earliest branch of the ruling House of the Mallas. This version of Jayasthiti Malla's ancestry cannot be taken seriously either, inasmuch as Jayadeva did not have a son of that name, and Jayasthiti Malla's own descendants laid pretentious and false claims to their descent from the Tirhutiya family of Harisiṃhadeva rather than from the early Mallas of Nepal itself. It has also been suggested that he might be a son of that shadowy figure Paśupati Malla who had made a brief appearance on the Bhadgaun scene, or that he was an obscure scion of the Khasya Malla family of western Nepal. None of these theories rest on any solid basis. The only hint we have of Jayasthiti Malla's origins comes from the *Gopālarājavaṃśāvalī* which says that he came from the South. It is possible that he came from Tirhut and this would explain why he was selected by Devaladevī and why his career was marked by a measure of immigration from Tirhut and by the very strong influence of the orthodox Jhā Brahmans of Tirhut.[1]

In 1361 Jayārjunadeva, son of Jayarājadeva, was crowned king after the death of his father. Like his father he was weak. He ruled directly over Bhonta and was recognised as king in Patan but the real power there was in the hands of the traditional aristocracy of Patan, the *mahāpātras*. His rule over Bhadgaun was nominal as long as Devaladevī lived but even this was later rejected. Jayasthiti Malla did not play a prominent role immediately after his marriage to Princess

Rājalladevī. His role became conspicuous only after the death of the feudatory chief, Anekarāma Mahātha in 1356 and of Regent Devaladevī in 1366. After her death Jayasthiti first cooperated with the king and his powerful minister Jayasiṃharāma, son of Anekarāma. The old feud between the two houses, however, soon flared up again when in 1370 Jayasthiti Malla won over the aristocracy of Patan and made a triumphant entry into the city on 28th April at the time of the Matsyendranāth festival. He rewarded local leaders, foremost of whom was Jayata Mūlamī whom he made his Prime Minister. Jayasiṃharāma tried to regain the lost ground and raised a rebellion against Jayasthiti in 1372 and again in 1374 but finally had to admit defeat. Despite all of this, Jayārjunadeva continued as king, but in 1380 Jayasthiti Malla and his minister Jayata Mahātha sent the king to Banepa on a pilgrimage. It was in fact an exile and exclusion from any political activity in the Valley. Some months later Jayārjunadeva made a last feeble attempt to regain his position and from the fort at Gokarna he took a force to Bhadgaun. He was easily defeated and confined to a room adjoining the Tripura palace in Bhadgaun where he died on 3rd February 1382. His death marked the end of the claims of the Bhonta lineage.

The official date of the beginning of Jayasthiti Malla's reign is 15th September 1382 when he officially accepted the homage and offerings of the assembled nobles in Bhadgaun. Jayasthiti Malla owed his throne to his own efforts and skill rather than to his position as the husband of Princess Rājalladevī of Bhadgaun, although naturally his position as Princess Rājalladevī's husband received due importance in the Bhadgaun documents. At Bhadgaun he ruled as Prince-Consort until the death of Rājalladevī in 1385. After her death, Bhadgaun was placed under one of Jayasthiti Malla's sons. After acquiring the Kingdom of Patan by conquest or by popular consent, through the submission of the seven *mahāpātras*, he was given the full royal title: *rājadhirājā parameśvara paramabhaṭṭāraka*, but only there. The Patan documents had used this title for him even before Rājalladevī's death. No Bhadgaun document, even after the death of Rājalladevī, ever gave him the full royal title.

Jayasthiti Malla restored a considerable measure of order and stability throughout the land after three quarters of a century of anarchy. It naturally took the rival feudatories some time to reconcile themselves to Jayasthiti Malla's supremacy. Nuwakot had overthrown the suzerainty of the Kathmandu Valley Kings and declared its independence. The Rāma family of Banepa tried to pick up the banner of the Bhonta house and carry it as their own but belatedly and reluctantly accepted Jayasthiti Malla's suzerainty. The feudal chiefs of Pharping were less aggressive, but this did not mean that they were more submissive. Jayasthiti Malla succeeded in controlling the refractory feudatories without entirely doing away with the hierarchical feudal system.

Jayasthiti Malla was a far-sighted ruler. He took a long-term view of the consolidation of Nepali society. He drew up a code of religious and social conduct with the help of five Brahmans from North and South India. Their names were: Kīrtinātha Upādhyāya Kānyakabuja, Rāghunātha Jhā Maithilī, Śrīnātha Bhaṭṭa, Mahīnātha Bhaṭṭa and Rāmanātha Jhā. His legal and social code aimed at consolidating Nepali society within the orthodox Hindu religious framework, with due regard and concessions for local conditions. The success of his policy is shown by the fact that the Newar society in the Valley to this day operates on the basis of his code, with only a few modifications. The distinctive feature of Jayasthiti Malla's code was that it did not lay stress on the traditional four classes (*varṇa*), but, in view of the existing conditions in Nepal, classified people into what may be called subcastes. It divided people into sixty-four subcastes and introduced detailed rules for marriage, interdining and drinking water, albeit in a relaxed form. Jayasthiti Malla's code also introduced a system of standard weights and measures and laid down rules for the use of pastures and the use of water for irrigation purposes.

A goddess known as Māneśvarī had been worshipped by the Licchavis and by their successors. Some time early in the fourteenth century, perhaps with the coming of the court of Harisiṃhadeva, a form of Dūrgā known as Taleju or Taleju Bhavānī found her way into the Valley perhaps as a result of contacts with the Ḍoya of Tirhut where she was the tutelar deity of Nānyadeva's dynasty. The two fused in the Valley and Jayasthiti Malla adopted Taleju as tutelary goddess in addition to Pashupatinath. Like Pashupatinath himself she thus forged a link joining all of these various dynasties. She was worshipped as a family deity by the successors of Jayasthiti Malla to the end of the Malla dynasty. Jayasthiti Malla, nonetheless, had a basically liberal outlook in matters of religion. He was devoted to Vishnu's popular incarnation as Rāma and encouraged the staging of plays that celebrated the incidents narrated in the *Rāmāyaṇa*. Some of his inscriptions also show his devotion to Shiva and Vishnu. Two persons, a Shaiva Swami named Śivadāsa and Dvijarāja Upādhyāya, were quite influential in his court. Jayasthiti Malla died on 5th September 1395.

Jayasthiti Malla had three sons, Jayadharma Malla (born 1367), Jayajyotir Malla (born 1373), and Jayakīrti Malla (born 1377). They ruled conjointly after their father's death with the eldest brother acting as their main representative. In documents from Bhadgaun the three brothers are listed as ruling jointly; in documents from Patan and Kathmandu, Jayadharma is given the full royal titles. Possibly, this arrangement was made to separate Jayasthiti Malla's own kingdom from his wife's inheritance of the principality of Bhadgaun.

It seems that even Jayasthiti Malla failed to repress the members of the Banepa family of Anekarāma. Jayasiṃharāma Vardhana Mahātha, son of Anekarāma, tried, after the death of Jayārjunadeva, to assert his old position as Lord-Protector of the realm. This was an attempt to vindicate the rights of the vacant throne of Bhonta, but it was doomed from the start. Gradually the Rāmas had to accept Jayasthiti Malla and develop a working relationship with him. They recognised Jayasthiti Malla but Jayasiṃharāma continued to hold Banepa as his seat of power as a sort of Prime Minister for the Bhonta principality with his younger brother, Madanarāma, bearing a similar title and residing at Palanchok. After the death of Jayasthiti Malla, Jayasiṃharāma and Madanarāma seem to have acted as senior and junior regents outside Bhadgaun. Their continued attempts to exert political influence and continued attempts to maintain a continuity with the extinct Bhonta dynasty helps to explain why they succeeded in being recognized as the rulers of Nepal by the Chinese Emperor. The Chinese Ming annals refer to Madanarāma and his sons and successors as Kings of Nepal. They state that Śaktisiṃharāma, son of Madanarāma, could not maintain the authority of his father and therefore retired to a valley to the east. In fact they were never kings of Nepal and their withdrawal to the east marks their returning to the only area they could call their own, the principality of Bhonta. Dhanavajra Vajracarya has reconstructed their genealogy as follows:

Jaitrarāma
|
Jyotirāma (fl. 1323)
|
Anekarāma (fl. 1332-1356)
|

Jayasiṃharāma (fl. 1360-1396)	Madanarāma (fl 1382-1399)
	Śaktisiṃharāma (fl.1382-1427)[2]

Jayajyotir Malla (1408-1428), who, of the three sons of Jayasthiti Malla, lived longest, eventually assumed the royal title as sole King of the whole of the Kathmandu Valley. He finally put an end to the influence of the Rāma family of Bhonta. For a while it seems that Patan became the seat of the royal Power and Bhadgaun was relegated to a position of secondary importance. However, the practice of appointing the Crown Prince as Governor of Bhadgaun recognised the importance of Bhadgaun as the place of origin of the royal family.

Jayajyotir was succeeded by his eldest son, Yakṣa Malla (1428-1482). His was a long and prosperous reign. Yakṣa Malla took advantage of a long period of stability and prosperity in his reign to extend the bounds of his kingdom. It is claimed that he conquered Mithila and extended his kingdom as far south as Gaya. He ensured the security of Nepal by defeating the hill rājās, including the king of Gorkha to the west. His kingdom extended to Bengal in the east and to the Ganges in the south. To the north his kingdom extended as far as Shekar Dzong in Tibet. A literary work by King Jagajyotir Malla of Bhadgaun (1614-1635) called *Narapatijayacaryā* (now preserved in the National Archives) gives this description of Yakṣa Malla's conquests. This account is, no doubt, exaggerated; but it is a fact that Yakṣa Malla added to the territory he had inherited from his father.

Yakṣa Malla set the precedent of entrusting the worship of Pashupati to the charge of Bhaṭṭa Brahmans from South India. He built the temple of Dattatreya at Bhadgaun and was probably responsible for the magnificent lattice window on the neighbouring Shaiva monastery, which is now famous as the 'Peacock Window'. The Newari language, which had already entered into the field of Nepali epigraphy in the time of Jayasthiti Malla, began to be even more widely used during the time of Yakṣa Malla and took the place formerly enjoyed by Sanskrit.

Yakṣa Malla's career marked the zenith of the power and glory of the Malla kings. After his death in 1482 the kingdom disintegrated. Some of the chronicles claim that Yakṣa Malla divided the kingdom among his sons. He did not, but this error has been so often repeated that it is important to review what actually happened and its causes. The disintegration was not a sudden event that can be simply blamed on the sons of Yakṣa Malla, much less on their father.

Divisive forces had been at work for at least two centuries before Yakṣa Malla became King, and they did not diminish during his reign. Internal strife and dissension had prevailed in Nepal since the days of Jayabhīmadeva (1258-71) and the struggle between the houses of Bhonta and Tripura. Throughout this time the situation was aggravated by external invasions. The invasions of the Kathmandu Valley by the Ḍoya, the Khasa Malla rulers of the Karnali region in the 13th and 14th centuries, and especially the invasion of Sultan Shamsuddin-Iliyas of Bengal in 1349 completely disrupted the social equilibrium of the country. A few strong personalities, like Jayarudra Malla and Anekarāma and some of the noble families like the Rāmas, the Mulamis and the Mahāthas fished in the troubled waters for their own self aggrandizement. The careers of Princess Nāyakadevī of Bhadgaun and her daughter, Princess Rajalladevī, show how dependent on courtiers, feudal officials and leading families, the rightful heirs to the throne, had become. There was an on-going tendency for cities where the king did not actually reside to go their own way under local rulers. After the death of Yakṣa Malla, Patan became in effect a city-state with its own rulers and remained so until the seventeenth century. The same process had begun in Kathmandu when one of Yakṣa Malla's sons went there as king to put a stop to it. This problem had existed during Yakṣa Malla's reign and he was able to subdue the local chieftains of Patan and Kathmandu, but he could not stop this tendency toward autonomy.

Yakṣa Malla had at least six sons: Rāya Malla, Ratna Malla, Raṇa Malla, Rāma Malla, Ari Malla, and Pūrṇa Malla. Besides these he had at least one daughter, Dharmavatī and one other son, Rāja Malla, who evidently predeceased his father. Already in 1462, the eldest son Rāya Malla, evidently tried to usurp royal status, but this attempt came to nothing. At the death of Yakṣa Malla the three senior brothers (Rāya, Ratna and Raṇa) ascended the throne and ruled jointly as had happened after the death of Jayasthiti Malla. By 1487 the three had taken their nephew Bhīma Malla (son of Dharmavatī) as an associate. Immediately a process of division set in with each of the three brothers claiming authority in a part of the kingdom. By 1484 Ratna Malla had established his rule in Kathmandu with his younger brother Ari Malla as an associate ruler. Later Ari Malla's son Indra Malla appears as an associate ruler, but after 1511 Ratna remains the sole ruler of Kathmandu. Rāya Malla was able to get himself recognised as the sole ruler of Bhadgaun and Raṇa Malla took hold of Bhonta with his capital in Banepa.

The eldest son, Rāya Malla, died in 1509 and Bhīma Malla disappeared from the scene. After this all pretense to unity was abandoned. Raṇa Malla returned from Banepa and acted for a time as regent to his nephews in Bhadgaun. When he died in 1529, without an heir, Banepa was reabsorbed by Bhadgaun. Patan went its own way. Until about 1520 it recognised the overlordship of the three kings and then of the king of Kathmandu. Finally Patan rejected the Mallas altogether and became formally independent under a king called Viṣṇusiṃha, one of the chief *mahāpātras* of Patan. It remained independent until it was conquered in about 1600 by Śivasiṃha of Kathmandu after whose death it became a separate kingdom with his grandson as king.[3] The perpetual strife and dissension caused by this division made the Kathmandu Valley an easy victim for the Gorkha conqueror, Pṛthvīnārāyaṇa Śāha, in 1768- 69.

NOTES

1. Jayasthiti Malla's Hindu orthodoxy and his attempts to impose this on the populace have become proverbial in the oral tradition. The later chronicles note his formulation of a strict Hindu code of law for the land mentioned below. At least two of the five Brahmans credited with the formulation of this law are Maithila Jhā Brahmans. A large number of literary works, mostly dramas, written in Maithili for the Bhadgaon court have also survived from this period.
2. Dhanavajra Vajracarya, 'Śaktiṣalī Bhārdār Rāmavarddhanaharū ra Tatkālik Nepāl', *Pūrṇima* 7:12-36; see also Petech, p. 152.
3. Śivasiṃha installed Hariharasiṃha his son as governor of Patan. He pre-deceased his father and at Sivasiṃha's death the kingdom was divided between Hariharasiṃha's two sons.

CHAPTER VII

A BRIEF ACCOUNT OF THE BETTER-KNOWN KINGDOMS IN MEDIEVAL NEPAL

Before we proceed with the history of the three Malla Kingdoms of the Kathmandu Valley, it may be apposite to add a note on the Malla dynasty of the Khasa Kingdom which we have already met in their incursions into the Valley, and a few words on the other kingdoms that dotted the area that is the modern state of Nepal. The present state or our knowledge does not enable us to write a comprehensive history of the whole of Nepal during the medieval period. The information that we possess is limited primarily to the Kathmandu Valley.

The Khasa Malla Dynasty of the Karnali Basin

In 1955 Prof. G. Tucci and Yogi Narharinath discovered the Dullu pillar and other inscriptions.[1] This discovery brought to light the rule of the Khasa Malla kings in the Karnali region. Their rule covered a period from the twelfth century through the fourteenth century. There were two Khasa dynasties at the beginning, one ruling Guge (Western Tibet) and the other Purang (modern Jumla and Surkhet). Guge consisted of a part of western Tibet known as Zanjun which, before the establishment of the Khasa dynasty, had its capital at Tsaparang and was ruled by the Tibetan Kings of the L De Family, who claimed their descent from the Lhasa kings. Guge, where one of the Khasa dynasties was initially based, was to the south of the Satlaj River. Purang, the seat of the other Khasa family, formed the south-eastern part of western Tibet with its capital at Tallakot. The two Khasa dynasties were merged when Pratāpa Malla (of the Purang-based Khasa dynasty), who had no male heir, gave his daughter Śakunamālā in marriage to Puṇya Malla (of the Guge based Khasa dynasty). Siñja, at the confluence of the two tributaries of the Karnali River in Jumla, became the capital of the united Khasa Kingdom. Pṛthvī Malla, son of Puṇya Malla and Śakunamālā, was probably the last king of the united Khasa Kingdom.

The Khasa Kingdom reached the height of its power during the reign of Pṛthvī Malla, who ruled over a large kingdom that consisted of Guge, Purang and the cis-Himalayan territory extending as far as Dullu to the south-west of Kashikot and Gorkha to the east.

The genealogical tree inscribed on the front side of the Dullu stone pillar names fifteen of the ancestral predecessors of Puṇya Malla, and shows him being followed by his son, Pṛthvī Malla, born of Śakunamālā, an heiress of the other Khasa dynasty. The family tree on the back of the same Dullu stone pillar shows Pratāpa Malla in the twelfth generation of his family line which begins with Nāgarāja, the founder of the Khasa dynasty at Purang, and mentions eleven of Pratāpa Malla's ancestral predecessors by name.

Among the predecessors of Pratāpa Malla were Kracalla and Aśokacalla, who ruled over an area that included Kumaun and Garhwal. Prof. Petech has determined the dates of the reign of Aśokacalla as being between A.D.1255 and 1278. Jitāri Malla, who invaded the Kathmandu Valley in 1288 and 1289, and Ripu Malla and Āditya Malla, who invaded it in 1312 and 1328 respectively, were the descendants of Aśokacalla and the immediate predecessors of Pratāpa Malla.

The discovery of the Malla dynasty in the Karnali region has certainly added to our knowledge of the medieval history of Nepal. It has not only enabled us to locate the origin of successive attacks on the Kathmandu Valley in the thirteenth and the fourteenth centuries, but has also made it clear, for the first time, that there were once other centres of power and civilisation in the present-day territory of Nepal itself. Although the Khasa kingdom of the Mallas in the west did not attain the same level of artistic and cultural development as the Kathmandu Valley of the Malla rulers, the achievements of the former were not insignificant by any count.

Ruins of Buddhist monasteries and Hindu temples show the prevalence of both Buddhism and Hinduism in the area. The co-existence of Hindu gods and goddesses with the Vajrayanic Siddhas (sages) reveals the same kind of religious and cultural synthesis that was obtained in the Kathmandu Valley under the Mallas. The images of both types show a fair level of artistic and sculptural development.

Trade was a main prop of an agricultural economy in hill areas which were unproductive compared to the fertile soil of the Kathmandu

Valley. The present-day Jumla-Dullu-Surkhet trail may, at that time, have been the main commercial highway for trans-Himalayan trade. Taklakot, the winter capital of the Khasa Malla dynasty, was the main gateway for Tibetan trade.

The Twenty-four Principalities (The Chaubise) and the Twenty-two Principalities (The Baise)

Following successive waves of the Muslim invasion of India launched by Mohammed of Ghanzi c. A.D. 999, immigrant Hindu chiefs from Rajasthan are said to have made their way into the hill areas of western Nepal. Over a period of time they carved out principalities for themselves and their progeny in the area which was largely inhabited by various indigenous tribes. The new rulers sought to trace their ancestry to some Indian Rajput clan or the other, but the links they tried to establish were, at best, tenuous. The Rajas of Piuthan boasted of their connection with the Chandelas, the Rajas of Khanchi and the Rajas of Dhurkot with the Medhasi clan, and the Rajas of Parvat, Galkot, Sallyan and Ghiring with the Samal clan. Nepali chronicles trace the ancestry of the Raja of Gorkha, along with the Rajas of Bhirkot, Nuwakot, Garahun, Satahun, Kaski and Lumjung, to a common Rajput stock of the lunar dynasty that had originally belonged to Chittor in Rajputana.

The Chaubise, or Twenty-four Principalities, and the Baise, or Twenty-two Principalities, together numbered forty-six principalities in all. Roughly speaking, the principalities in the Gandaki region of central Nepal were known as the Chaubise and those in the Karnali region of western Nepal as the Baise. However, it was not possible to draw a strict boundary-line between the geographical areas comprising the Chaubise and the Baise states inasmuch as natural frontiers did not exist between them. These two categories of hill states did not represent collective political entities nor did they form permanent alliances of any kind. All the forty-six principalities were independent and sovereign, for all practical purposes, and were constantly engaged in fighting one another, unable to evolve a system for regulating relations among themselves.

There are no fixed or permanent lists of the Twenty-four and Twenty-two Principalities. Some of them, especially those geographically situated in the border region, are named on both lists. Parvat (Malebam), Galkot, Piuthan, Khungrikot, and Bhingrikot generally occurred on both lists because their boundaries adjoined the Chaubise and Baise geographical divisions.

Most of these kingdoms lay entirely in the hills, but a few of them had land either in the tarai, the lowland plains adjoining what is now Bihar and Uttar Pradesh, or low land behind the first low range of hills—called the 'Inner Tarai' (*bhitrī madeś*) in Nepal and Doon Valleys in India. Possession of tarai or Inner Tarai land made the difference between a 'rich' state and a 'poor' state, for the elephants and fish, and above all, the flat, fertile land which provided rich revenue, enabled the state to rise above the subsistence level. The only kingdoms of these forty-six which had tarai lands were Tanahuñ, Palpa and Piuthan, among the Twenty-four Principalities, and Salyan, Dang-Deukhuri and Dullu among the Twenty-two Principalities.

The Twenty-four Principalities

Francis Buchanan Hamilton lists the Chaubise or Twenty-four Principalities as follows:[2]

1. Piuṭhan	7. Khanchi	13. Bhirkot	19. Ghiring
2. Malebam (Parvat)	8. Gulmi	14. Nuwakot	20. Tanahun
3. Galkot	9. Palpa	15. Kaski	21. Lamjung
4. Isma	10. Garahun	16. Dhor	22. Gorkha
5. Dhurkot	11. Paiyun	17. Gajarkot	23. Tarki
6. Argha	12. Satahun	18. Rising	24. Musikot

According to information available to Hamilton in 1803-4, temporary alliances had existed among various states along the following lines:

1. Lamjung led the alliance composed of itself, Tanahun and Kaski, but independently of Lamjung, Tanahun had the backing of Dhor and Kaski that of Satahun.
2. Bhirkot headed the group composed of itself, Gajarkot, Rising, Ghiring, Argha, Khanchi and Gulmi.
3. Palpa was the leader of a group consisting of itself, Gajarkot, Rising, Ghiring, Argha, Khanchi and Gulmi.
4. Malebam formed an alliance with Galkot.
5. Piuthan led the alliance composed of itself, Musikot and Isma along with the two petty chiefs of Khungrikot and Bhingrikot,

who, though surrounded by the Chaubise, were not included among them.[3]

The ruling houses of the eight Chaubise principalities, Bhirkot, Garahun, Satahun, Nuwakot, Kaski, Dhor and Gorkha came of the same stock and were branches of the Khān family that had originally ruled from Bhirkot. The original family of the Khāns split into the sub-branches that later called themselves Śāha and Śāhī. As the ruling house of Gorkha later became the ruling dynasty of Nepal, its links with the Rajput clan of Chittor, however tenuous, received a good deal of attention. However, the circumstances described in the chronicles do not agree with the historical facts.

Some of the chronicles trace the ancestry of the Ruling House of Gorkha to one Bhūpati Rāṇāji Rao of Chittor. According to these sources, his son, Fateh Rāṇā refused to give his daughter in marriage to Akbar, the great Mughal Emperor of India, and invited his wrath. Fateh Rāṇā lost his life and kingdom in a fierce battle with Akbar's army. His two brothers, Udaṃbara and Manmatha, continued to offer resistance to the Mughal Emperor from Udaipur and Ujjain respectively. It was Manmatha's son, Bhūpāl Rāṇājī, who entered the central Himalayan region and reached Ridi, near Palpa, in 1495. This contradicts the facts for Akbar was born in A.D. 1542.

Other chronicles trace the circumstances of the flight of Bhūpati and Manmatha to the conquest of Chittor by Alauddin Khilji in A.D. 1303. However, the chronicles generally agree that a descendant of Manmatha, named Bhūpāl, went to Palpa, by way of Ridi, from somewhere in India and settled down in the village of Lasargha, situated on the Waigha Ridge on the left bank of the River Kali Gandaki. Bhūpāl's son, Jain Khān, lived and died at Lasargha, but Sūrya Khān, Jain Khān's son, proceeded to Bhirkot and settled down in a village called Khilung, on the bank of the river Andhi Khola. Of the two sons of Sūrya Khān, Khancha, the elder son, acquired control of Bhirkot, Garahun, Satahun and Dhor and became the king of the area. The younger son, Micha Khān, established his rule in Nuwakot and one of his descendants, named Kulmardan, adopted the title of Śāha. Some of the later descendants of Micha Khān subsequently seized control of Kaski and made it their seat of government. Meanwhile, Lamjung adopted as its king a prince of the family named Yaśobrahma. Dravya Śāha, who acquired the Kingdom of Gorkha by conquest was Yaśobrahma's second son.

Palpa was the most important of the Twenty-four Principalities as it had acquired, on lease from the Muslim rulers in Oudh (Awadh), extensive tracts of land in the Tarai. Butaul, at the feet of the mountains surrounding Palpa, was a thriving centre of trade and served as a source of commercial supplies, not only to Palpa but also to a large section of the hinterland in Central Nepal. Palpa was a much bigger kingdom until Argha, Khanchi and Gulmi seceded to become independent principalities. Branches of the Sena dynasty of Palpa ruled the independent kingdoms of Makwanpur and Tanahuñ also. The Makwanpur branch subsequently divided and created the independent kingdoms of Chaudandi and Vijayapur in the eastern Nepal Tarai and hills.

Northwest of Palpa was the principality of Parvat which was sometimes called Malebam after its ruler of that name. Its boundary touched Jumla in the west and Kaski in the east, and the principality also included areas in the trans-Himalayan region in the north.

The Twenty-two Principalities

The Twenty-two Principalities in the Karnali region were once part of the kingdom of the united Khasa Malla dynasty, with its summer capital at Siñja and its winter capital at Tallakot. Jumla proved to be the most powerful of the Twenty-two Principalities and controlled one or two principalities that lay in the Gandaki region. The principality of Mustang, founded in the 15th century and situated in the trans-Himalayan region behind the Annapurna and Dhaulagiri range, came under the sway of Jumla in 1760 after intermittent warfare extending over a period of three centuries.

The Twenty-two Principalities that lie between the western-most boundary of Piuthan and the Mahakali River are listed as follows:[4]

1. Jumla	7. Jajarkot	13. Musikot	19. Kalagaun
2. Doti	8. Baphi	14. Khungrikot	20. Gotam
3. Bajhang	9. Dang-Deukhuri	15. Bhingrikot	21. Goriakot
4. Acham	10. Phalebang	16. Jahari	22. Gajur
5. Thallara	11. Rolpa	17. Chilli	
6. Dailekh	12. Rukumkot	18. Malnetta	

The Kingdoms in the Tarai

In the eastern Nepal tarai, there were as many as three kingdoms by the eighteenth century. The kingdom of Makwanpur, situated to the south of the Kathmandu Valley, included the present tarai districts of Bara, Parsa and Rautahat. It was ruled by the Sena rulers who belonged to one of the sub-branches of the Sena dynasty of Palpa.

The kingdom of Chaudandi contained the eastern tarai districts of Saptari, Siraha, Mahottari, Dhanusa, Sarlahi and also the eastern hill districts of Okhaldhunga and Bhojpur. East of the kingdom of Chaudandi was the powerful and extensive Kingdom of Vijayapur, which was ruled by a sub-branch of the Sena dynasty of Palpa, with the title of 'Hindūpati' or 'Overlord of the Hindus'. The kingdom of Vijayapur once contained within it the territory of Chaudandi. After the division, Vijayapur included the tarai districts of Morang, Sunsari, and Jhapa. In addition, it also exercised control over the far-eastern hill districts of Dhankuta, Panchtar, Taplejung, Therathum and Sankhuwa-Sabha. Although the Sena rulers of Makwanpur, Chaudandi and Vijayapur were originally connected with the Sena dynasty of Palpa and also with each other, these dynastic links seldom served any political purpose. However, the novel feature of the political set-up in Vijayapur was the acceptance of its ruler's authority by the autonomous Kirāti units in the hills in return for the appointment of a hill-based Kirāti minister by the Hindu kings in the tarai.

At the present time there is not sufficient information to sketch a connected outline of the historical developments within the various principalities of the different regions. We must, therefore, be content with this brief summary in our account of how they were all gradually incorporated in the expanding area dominated by the Gorkhalis, which eventually became the modern Kingdom of Nepal.

Banepa

We have already traced the development of the principality of Banepa or Bhonta with its royal line of '—deva' kings and the powerful ministers of the Rāma family. Banepa became one of the three independent kingdoms, along with Bhadgaun and Kathmandu, that arose out of the disintegration of the kingdom of the Kathmandu Valley after the death of Yakṣa Malla. Raṇa Malla, one of the sons of Yakṣa Malla, became the king of Banepa. He later returned to Bhadgaun to act as regent for his nephews and at his death Banepa was re-absorbed by the kingdom of

Bhadgaun. There is some evidence that it became separate again under one Keśava Malla who appears to be a ruler of Banepa in A.D.1539. From the time of Jagatprakāśa Malla (1644-1673) of Bhadgaun the records clearly show Banepa being administered as a part of Bhadgaun.

Nuwakot

Nuwakot was a feudal principality situated about thirty miles to the west of Kathmandu. Its chiefs also ruled over the Kathmandu Valley in the early medieval times. Like so many of these feudal principalities, it attempted to assert its independence when the kings of the Valley were weak but officially remained under the Malla kings of the Valley. In the late Malla period it was the western outpost of the kingdom of Kathmandu and the first place attacked by the King of Gorkha.

Dolakha

Dolakha, which lies to the east of the Kathmandu Valley and was settled by Newars from the Valley, was for long a very important centre. Most of the trading expeditions going to Tibet passed through Dolakha. Dhanavajra Vajracarya and Tek Bahadur Shrestha have collected important documents from Dolakha which prove that an independent kingdom was established there for a century.[5]

During King Yakṣa Malla's powerful reign the Dolakha region was governed by a feudatory ruler named Kīrti Siṃha. His last known date is A.D.1474. Kīrti Siṃha's son, Udhava Deva, became independent of the central government during the period when Yakṣa Malla's successors were divided into various groups. Thus in 1491 Udhava Deva appears as a semi-independent ruler of Dolakha, though he was still loosely connected to the centre once again some years later.

Nanda Deva, Ujota Deva and Govinda Deva were the successors of Udhava Deva. Next comes the important name of Indra Siṃha Deva who probably began to rule in A.D.1534. He issued a silver coin sometime before 1548 and thus became the first ruler in Nepali history to issue a silver *mohara* coin. Indra Siṃha's successors maintained their political identity in Dolakha up to 1595 when the king of Kathmandu, Śiva Siṃha Malla, occupied Dolakha and placed it under his rule.

Conclusion

After the Licchavi period, Nepal became divided into several kingdoms. The Kathmandu Valley itself split into a number of political units. There were at least three independent kingdoms—Kathmandu, Bhadgaun and Patan—by the end of the fifteenth century. Even Banepa and Nuwakot to the east and the west respectively were able to assert their independence occasionally. In the Karnali region, the powerful kingdom of the Khasa Mallas came into existence by the twelfth century. It is not yet clear just when this kingdom disintegrated but by the sixteenth century there were at least forty-six principalities in the western part of Nepal. These included the Twenty-four Principalities in the Gandaki region of central Nepal, and the Twenty-two Principalities in the Karnali region. As we have seen, in the south and south-east, the kingdoms of Makwanpur, Chaudandi and Vijayapur emerged under the the several branches of the Sena dynasty of Palpa. Chaudandi and Vijayapur, which respectively had their capitals in Saptari and Morang in the tarai, also included the tribal communities of the Kirātīs in the eastern hill region. Although the above states nominally recognised the supremacy of several of the more powerful among them, the Twenty-four and the Twenty-two Principalities were virtually independent and engaged in continual warfare. The chaotic state of relations among these states prepared the way for the rise of the Gorkhalis and, ultimately, for the formation of the present-day state of Nepal.

NOTES

1. See G. Tucci, *Preliminary Report on Two Scientific Expeditions in Nepal*, Roma, Instituto Italiano per il Medio ed Estremo Oriente, 1956, on which the data for this section is based.
2. Francis Buchanan Hamilton, *An Account of the Kingdom of Nepal*, Mānjuśri Publishing House, New Delhi, 1971, p. 238.
3. *Ibid.*, pp. 239-40.
4. *Ibid.*, p. 268 ff.
5. Dhanavajra Vajracarya and Tek Bahadur Shrestha, *Dholakhāko Aitihāsik Rūp-rekhā*, Kathmandu, 2031 V.S.

CHAPTER VIII

THE KINGDOM OF KATHMANDU (c.1484-1768)

Ratna Malla, who had become King of Kathmandu by 1482 following the disintergation of the central Kingdom of the Kathmandu Valley, was an energetic, ambitious and unscrupulous ruler. For some time he ruled over Patan also. He increased his authority by suppressing the rebellious Thakuri feudatories of Nuwakot and other areas, and with the assistance of Palpa, repulsed the Bhotia intrusions.

During Ratna Malla's rule, Brahmans from South India and Mithila became prominent in the affairs of the court to the exclusion of local Hindu and Buddhist priests, but he did not neglect the worship and care of traditional goddesses. He circulated copper coins and exploited local copper mines for the purpose.

Ratna Malla died in the year A.D.1520 and was succeeded by his son, Sūrya Malla (1520-1529). The later chronicles note an invasion of Nepal by one Mukunda Sena and give various dates for this invasion such as A.D.1110 and A.D.1258. This had long vexed Nepali historians and much effort was expended in trying to identify this king. A notation found on a manuscript copy of the *Nāradasmṛti* and recently published by Maheshraj and Dineshraj Pant notes two invasions of Mukunda Sena in the year A.D.1526 and in the previous year. This fits, for at that time we know from other sources that Mukunda Sena was the king of Palpa. He attacked various places in the Valley and at one time had both Kathmandu and Patan surrounded. This happened, therefore, in the time of Sūrya Malla.[1]

Sūrya Malla died in 1529 and was succeeded by his son Amara (Narendra) Malla (1529-1560). Both names for this king occur in various documents, and for a long time scholars thought that Amara and Narendra were different kings. It is now clear that they are one and the same. Amara Malla was a man of religious temperament. He patronised the dance of the goddess Harisiddhi and also revived other religious dances such as Mana Maijū, Haricoka Devī, Pacalī Bhairava, Navadūrgā, Bhadrakālī, and Kaṅkeśvarī.

Upon the death of Amara Malla, Mahendra Malla became king and ruled until his death in 1574. Mahendra Malla built the royal palace in Kathmandu on the model of the Bhadgaun palace, and in 1563 built the Taleju Temple within the palace complex. He issued silver *mohara* coins, and for a long time Nepali silver coins were so associated with his name that they were called *mahendramallīs*. The first Nepali coin found in Tibet was that of Bhūpatindra Malla, king of Bhadgaun (1696-1722). This led both Sylvain Levi and Walsh to dismiss as a myth the accounts of the minting of coins by Mahendra Malla for circulation in Tibet, but since these silver *mohara* coins have now been found the theory is untenable. Following in the footsteps of Jayasthiti Malla, the illustrious King of the Kathmandu Valley, Mahendra Malla also laid down a code for regulating the social, economic and religious life and conduct of his subjects.

Mahendra Malla was succeeded by his eldest son Sadāśiva Malla (1574-c. 1578). Sadāśiva was notorious for his profligacy, and his half-brother Śivasiṃha was soon claiming the kingship. Finally this opposition from his brother and a general public outcry forced him to flee Kathmandu and seek shelter in Bhadgaun where he seems to have died in A.D.1581. Śivasiṃha commenced to rule about 1578. He repaired the Swayambhu stūpa and the temple of Changunarayan. Śivasiṃha was an ambitious king. At the turn of the century he seized Patan where the successors of Viṣṇusiṃha had maintained an independent kingdom since the time of Ratna Malla and the disintegration of Yaksa Malla's kingdom. After this he planned to expand eastward and occupied Dolakha where the Deva dynasty had been ruling an independent kingdom for a century. In Patan he had installed his son Hariharasiṃha as governor. When Hariharasiṃha died his wife conspired to have one of her sons, Siddhinarasiṃha, installed as governor. When Śivasiṃha died in A.D.1617 he was succeeded by his elder grandson Lakṣmīnarasiṃha and the two grandsons split the kingdom. Thus Patan retained its independence, but now under a Malla king, no longer under its own rulers.

Lakṣmīnarasiṃha lost some of his territory to his brother as the area east of the Bagmati River was incorporated into Patan. Lakṣmīnarasiṃha, being a man of peaceful and quiet disposition, took no steps to regain this territory. He finally concluded a treaty of peace and friendship with his brother, Siddhinarasiṃha, King of Patan. Lakṣmīnarasiṃha himself strictly adhered to the treaty, but later he became insane and his son, Pratāpa Malla, captured some of the forts of Patan.

Because of his father's insanity Pratāpa Malla assumed effective power in the kingdom being formally recognised as king in A.D.1641, long before his father's death in 1659. Pratāpa Malla had a very wise and experienced minister in one of his distant relatives of the royal family, one Kājī Bhīma Malla. Kājī Bhīma Malla conquered Dolakha, on the Kathmandu-Lhasa route, and also led a military expedition into Tibet. He overran Kuti and advanced toward Shigatse. Tibet sued for peace and a treaty was signed under which Kathmandu was given joint authority with Tibet in the border towns of Kuti and Kerung. Newari merchants of the Kathmandu Valley were permitted to establish thirty-two trading houses in Tibet. This facilitated imports of silver and gold. Bhīma Malla arranged with the Tibetan authorities that escheat property of Nepali traders in Tibet should accrue to the Nepal (i.e. Kathmandu) government. These arrangements led to a considerable increase in the volume of Nepal's trade with Tibet.

The success of Kājī Bhīma Malla's expedition to Tibet provoked jealousy among the other courtiers. Hence two of his rivals, Mayasiṃha and Mahādeva Ojhā, hatched a successful plot to assassinate him. The story of the treachery worked on Bhīma Malla has become proverbial. At his funeral his wife uttered a curse (*satīko sarāp*) and this has become a proverb the import of which is: 'Selfless service to the country is ill-requited in Nepal'.

In the first half of the seventeenth century, as a result of the struggle for power among the various Tibetan Buddhist sects, Tibet was virtually in a state of anarchy. At this time, Nepal had two strong and ambitious kings: Rāma Śāha of Gorkha (c. 1606-1633) and Pratāpa Malla of Kathmandu (1641-1674). It was only natural that they should try to take advantage of Tibet's weakness to control the main trade routes between Nepal and Tibet. Incursions across the Tibetan border by Rāma Śāha and Pratāpa Malla probably took place in A.D.1630 and 1649 respectively. Rāma Śāha's conquests in Tibet threatened the Valley's important trade route to Kerung. This necessitated immediate and bold action on the part of the Kathmandu Valley to preserve its near-monopoly in Nepal-Tibet trade. Hence Pratāpa Malla's determined and successful military campaign against Dambara Śāha, King of Gorkha (c. 1635-1642) at a time when Dambara Śāha was helping the Patan king, Siddhinarasiṃha Malla. Pratāpa Malla thus extended his sway over Kerung and Kuti. From the accounts of the Capuchin missionaries who passed through Nepal on their way to India and Europe from Tibet, we know that the commercial goods and products of Nepal were very much in demand in Tibet. To ensure Nepal's interests in the entrepot trade between India and Tibet, Pratāpa Malla also attacked Makwanpur, to the south-east, with the joint support of Patan and Bhadgaun, and imposed terms on it.

By conquering some of the forts of Patan, Pratāpa Malla forced Patan to sue for peace. Then with the help of Patan's king, Śrīnivāsa Malla, he invaded Bhadgaun. The war continued for two years, almost without a break. Pratāpa Malla carried the war to the very heart of Bhadgaun and inflicted considerable damage on its buildings. He thus forced King Jagatprakāśa Malla of Bhadgaun to accept his terms for peace.

Pratāpa Malla was a proud and ambitious king. He wanted to leave his mark on history. Inscriptions of hymns composed by him are found within the precincts of the temples of Pashupatinath and Guhyeshwari, in the Buddhist shrine of Swayambhu and in many other places. The still extant Rānī Pokharī tank in Kathmandu was built by King Pratāpa Malla, towards the end of his rule, to console his queen after the death of their son Cakravartendra Malla. Water from holy places was poured into it so that the people might bathe and offer oblations to their gods and ancestors. He constructed many temples in the memory of his deceased wives. However, his primary motive in performing these acts was probably the perpetuation of his own memory.

Pratāpa Malla's vain-glorious nature was apparent in everything he did. He assumed the title of 'Chief Among Poets' (*kavindra*), despite the fact that his poetry was of a rather mediocre quality. Poets and sycophants satisfied his vanity by paying tribute to him not only as a successful poet but also as an accomplished painter. He was extolled as 'proficient in all branches of learning and adept in the use of all kinds of weapons'. He put up a multi-script tablet of jumbled words in various languages and scripts, which did not make any sense and which was intended to be a concrete and lasting proof of his linguistic proficiency. This tablet can still be seen at the Hanūmān Ḍhokā Palace.

Though his knowledge of other subjects was also superficial, he was a patron of scholars and men of religion who gathered at his court from distant places in India. He sought to profit by their company and add to his own knowledge of various branches of learning. He was especially interested in Tantric lore and practices. Among the scholars in permanent attendance at his court was a tantric philosopher by the name of Jñānānanda from the Deccan, a Maharastrian magic teacher named Lambakarṇa Bhaṭṭa, a Tirhutiya logician by the name of Narasiṃha

Ṭhākur, a Tibetan Lama named Shāmarpa and a local scholar-priest by the name of Jāmana Gubhāju.

At the temple of Pashupatinath, in a religious ceremony called *tuladāna*, Pratāpa Malla once gave away in charity one hundred horses and his own weight in gold, silver, pearls and coral. It may be noted that the practice of giving away one's own weight in valuables as an act of charity was also prevalent in those days among the Mughal rulers of India. A drama called *Gīta-digaṃvaram* (a hymn to Mahādeva), was performed for the entertainment of those assembled to watch Pratāpa Malla make his religious donation. The drama, which bestowed fulsome praise on King Pratāpa Malla, was specially written by one Vaṃśamaṇi Jhā for the purpose. Most of the Malla kings sponsored religious activities for the recreation and entertainment of their subjects. New religious processions, dances and plays provided healthy amusements which also served as vehicles of popular education. Though the later chronicles credit Pratāpa Malla with starting the White Matsyendranath procession in Kathmandu, it is clear he did not. There are references to the festival as early as A.D.1627 in the reign of his father. Yet it is clear that he took part in this festival and patronised it. Thus, he shared with other kings of Nepal his devotion to both Hinduism and Buddhism.

Pratāpa Malla introduced reforms in the administration of justice. He imparted greater responsibility to the judge in deciding cases and permitted trial by ordeal only for capital offences. He was proud of his marriage connection with the state of Kuch Bihar, Another wife, Rājamatī, was a princess of the Karnata dynasty of Tirhut. He also married Pārvatī, daughter of the Raja of Bhagavatipur, and Lālamatī, daughter of the Raja of Mahottari. He had a large number of other wives and mistresses as well.

Pratāpa Malla's fondness for women and for magical practices and incantations was, in part, a result of his interest in Tantric yoga and its practices. Chronicles relate how, by virtue of his courage and the power of his magic, he once removed an ancient book written in the blood of snakes (*nāga*) from the inner sanctum of the Śāntipūra shrine at Swayambhu and thus relieved the people of a prolonged drought. A still extant painting portrays and describes the scene. The king and his court had assembled to witness the removal of the book from the inner sanctum, where no one had dared enter for centuries, by the Vajrācārya priest in charge of the shrine. The priest was too terrified to enter so the king agreed to accompany him. As they stepped across the threshold the Vajrācārya fainted dead away and Pratāpa went on alone.

Legend ascribes even his death in 1674 to supernatural causes. When he was watching the Harisiddhi dance, he found a beautiful girl sitting next to him and made advances toward her. Alas, the girl turned out to be the goddess Harisiddhi herself, and Pratāpa Malla died instantly as he had incurred her displeasure.

Pratāpa Malla had several sons by his innumerable wives. He sought to make his favourite sons his heirs apparent. Unfortunately, his dearest son, Cakravartindra Malla, died during his lifetime. His eldest son also predeceased him. As a result of his manipulations and favouritism, considerable misunderstanding arose on the question of succession after his death. Mahīpatendra Malla, whom Pratāpa had wanted to be his successor, had finally to yield to his half-brother Nṛpendra Malla (1674-1680), as a result of a consensus reached between the royal family of Kathmandu and King Śrīnivāsa Malla of Patan. Śrīnivāsa Malla lent the services of an experienced minister named Chikutī to assist his grand-nephew Nṛpendra. With the help of Chikutī, Nṛpendra Malla ruled for six years without incident. He died, however, in A.D.1680 without leaving any male issue.

Nṛpendra was succeeded by his brother Parthivendra Malla (1680-1687) who replaced Chikutī with one Raut Bhakuta. Parthivendra resembled his father, Pratāpa Malla, in some ways. He erected statues of himself, his wives, his mother and his son. He claimed the conquest of Sindhuli, fifty miles to the south-east, and called himself 'The King of Poets' (*kavirāja*).

When he died in 1687 Parthivendra left the throne to an eight year old son, Bhūpālendra Malla (1687-1700). With the support of Bhūpālendra's mother, regent Queen Ṛddhilakṣmī, one Lakṣmīnārāyaṇa Jośi became Chief Minister and the supreme authority in the realm. He even had his name inscribed on the reverse of Bhūpālendra's coins. As Lakṣmīnārāyaṇa had come into prominence after the removal of Chikutī as Minister during the time of King Parthivendra, he considered the existence of men like Chikutī as a potential threat to his newly acquired power. Lakṣmīnārāyaṇa finally had Chikutī and one Vaṃśidhara, another prominent courtier from Patan, assassinated with the aid of two men called Kanu Ojhā and Badala Ojhā. These two men were members of the notorious family of Mahādeva Ojhā, who had in similar circumstances, assassinated Kājī Bhīma Malla during Pratāpa Malla's reign. Having eliminated his potential rivals in this manner, Lakṣmīnārāyaṇa Jośi carried on the administration with a strong and heavy hand, temporarily dominating even the kings of Bhadgaun and Patan. His overbearing manner, combined with widespread rumours about a liaison with Regent Queen Ṛddhilakṣmī excited the wrath and jealousy of the entire court as well as of the rulers of Bhadgaun and Patan. As a result he was assassinated in A.D. 1690.

After the assassination of Lakṣmīnārāyaṇa, Regent Queen Ṛddhilakṣmī continued to be the power behind the throne. However, King Bhūpālendra Malla soon began to have differences with his mother and, as he matured, he took over the entire administration. The young man was said to be fond of military activity, but his military campaigns, directed mainly against Patan and Bhadgaon, did not result in any territorial gains. He died in A.D.1700 at the age of twenty-one while on a pilgrimage to Varanasi and Ayodhya.

Bhūpālendra was succeeded by another minor, his four year old son, Bhāskara Malla (A.D.1700-1722). The dowager Queen Bhūvanalakṣmī functioned as Regent. At that time Patan also had a minor on the throne following the death of Yoganarendra Malla. Bhadgaun alone had, in Bhūpatindra Malla, an adult King with some experience of administration. Regent Queen Bhūvanalakṣmī maintained friendly relations with Bhadgaun without surrendering her independence in any way. At the same time, she maintained peace with Patan.

At this point our sources lead us into confusion for there are several references after 1714 to a king of Kathmandu in this period calling himself Mahendrasiṃha. Much effort has gone into trying to determine who this man was and where he came from. In fact Mahendrasiṃha is most probably another name for Bhūpālendra Malla. One of the later chronicles, the Bhāṣāvaṃśāvalī actually states that Mahendrasiṃha's earlier name was Bhāskara.[2] Much more important, though, than a single reference in an often unreliable chronicle, is a series of overlapping contemporary sources which refer to the King of Kathmandu alternately now as Bhāskara now as Mahindrasiṃha with Bhāskara Malla being referred to as late as 1719. These were first pointed out several years ago by Shankar Man Rajvamsi.[3] Furthermore, we have abundant material from court records of this period on the births, initiations, marriages, etc. of members of the royal family of Kathmandu. No Mahendrasiṃha is mentioned in these records.

Bhāskara-Mahendrasiṃha also served as king of Patan from A.D.1710- 1715. He permitted Muslim musicians, perfumers and bangle dealers to settle in Kathmandu. He even appointed a Muslim as his minister, but this resulted in a popular uprising in the course of which all but five of the Muslim settlers were slaughtered. The date of Bhāskara Malla's death is not certain but by 1722 his successor was ruling.

The year 1722 saw new rulers in all three of the kingdoms of the Kathmandu Valley: Jagajjaya Malla in Kathmandu, Ranajita Malla in Bhadgaun and Yogaprakāśā Malla in Patan. Jagajjaya Malla (c. 1722-1733) had been adopted by Bhāskara-Mahendrasiṃha as his successor. He was the son of one Kumudinī Devī, daughter of Mahīpatendra Malla, a son of King Pratāpa Malla. Mahīpatendra Malla had been deprived of his right of succession and died a fugitive during the reign of his brother Parthivendra Malla. Jagajjaya inscribed the names of both his mother, Kumudinī, and his maternal grandfather, Mahīpatendra, on his coins. He also received tribute from the kings of Morang and Makwanpur.

Rajendra Malla, Jagajjaya's eldest son and heir apparent, died before his father, but Jagajjaya had four other sons: Jayaprakāśā Malla, Rājyaprakāśā Malla, Narendraprakāśā Malla and Candraprakāśā Malla. In 1722 Jagajjaya Malla granted permission to Capuchin missionaries to work in Kathmandu. He fought with King Bhūpatīndra Malla of Bhadgaun very often, but was at peace with Patan, because his daughter was married to the king of Patan, Viṣṇu Malla.

Jayaprakāśā Malla ascended the throne in 1734 after his father's death. Even before he became king, Khasa military officers from the hills who served in his army had shown their dislike for him. They expressed their preference for Jagajjaya's second son, Rājyaprakāśā. Naturally, therefore, Jayaprakāśā looked upon these officers with suspicion. As if to confirm his suspicions, they soon hatched a plot to dethrone him. They induced his younger brother, Narendraprakāśā, to declare himself an independent king in the north-eastern part of the kingdom, i.e. in Sankhu and Changu. It took Jayaprakāśā four months to put down this rebellion.

If Jayaprakāśā did not trust his Khasa officers from the hills, he was no more satisfied with the nobles of his father's time, like Shuka Bha. He appointed one Ranavira Thapa, from the eastern hill district of Palanchok as Chief Officer of the court in place of Shuka Bha. In 1744 Pṛthvīnārāyaṇa Śāha of Gorkha, who had ascended the throne in 1742, wrested Nuwakot from Kathmandu. When Kāśirāma Thāpā and other Thāpā officers of Palanchok failed to recover Nuwakot from Gorkha, Jayaprakāśā suspected them of being in league with Pṛthvīnārāyaṇa. Kāśirāma Thāpā was punished with death along with his associates. This turned the influential Thāpā family of Palanchok against Jayaprakāśā. Kāśirāma Thāpā's younger brother, Parśurāma Thāpā, therefore went over to Pṛthvīnārāyaṇa Śāha.

Jayaprakāśā also ordered the execution of an old officer called Dati. At this, Dati's brother, Taudika, sought asylum in the Patan court. Jayaprakāśā thus made enemies of both the Khasa and the Newari officers of his court. He began to rely more and more on his Maithili Brahman advisors, and on the troops recruited in the Indian plains and the distant hills of Doti.

King Raṇajita Malla (1722-1769) of Bhadgaun was openly hostile to Jayaprakāśā Malla. Unwittingly, Raṇajita Malla was cooperating in Pṛthvīnārāyaṇa Śāha's move to blockade the Valley. Jayaprakāśā was not even on good terms with his own brother, King Rājyaprakāśā Malla of Patan, because the latter had given refuge to disgruntled officials of the Kathmandu court like Taudika.

Gorkha's troops occupied Sankhu and Gokarna, near Kathmandu, in 1746 and Jayaprakāśā Malla suffered tremendous loss of face as a result. Naturally there was great unrest among the people of the Kathmandu Valley. Ranajita Malla of Bhadgaun kept quiet because of his prior understanding with Pṛthvīnārāyaṇa Śāha. Patan took quick action and rushed troops to relieve Gokarna and Sankhu. These troops also succeeded in dethroning Jayaprakāśā Malla and replacing him with his minor son, Jyotiprakāśā Malla, under the regency of his mother, Dayāvati from 1746-1752. Taudika became minister of the court in Kathmandu and he forced the Gorkhalis to retreat beyond the Sanga pass.

Jayaprakāśā remained in exile for at least four years with a few loyal officers. His resumption of power was facilitated by the scandalous affair of his wife, Dayāvatī, with an officer called Garuḍadhvaja. Taudika withdrew his support from Dayāvatī, and Garuḍadhvaja was assassinated. After regaining power, Jayaprakāśā imprisoned his wife as a punishment for her complicity in the plot against him. Taudika once again went into exile.

After Jayaprakāśā regained his throne in 1752, he tried his best to counter the moves of Pṛthvīnārāyaṇa Śāha designed to weaken the defense of the Kathmandu Valley. With the support of Bhadgaun and Patan, Jayaprakāśā went to the assistance of Kirtipur when it was attacked by the Gorkhali troops in 1757 and 1764. On both occasions the Gorkhali attacks were repulsed successfully. Pṛthvīnārāyaṇa's strategy against the Valley had much advanced by 1764. In 1762 he had attacked Makwanpur. This made it possible for him to block the southern entrance to the Kathmandu Valley. Even before Gorkha's 1758 treaty with Kathmandu which negotiated the sharing of the revenue from trade with Tibet, Pṛthvīnārāyaṇa had acquired full control of Kabhrepalanchok and

Sindhupalchok, on the main trade route to Lhasa through the Kuti pass. Thus the Kathmandu Valley was blockaded from all sides.

Despite Jayaprakāśā's repeated pleas for unity in the face of Gorkha's menace, the nobles of Patan invited Pṛthvīnārāyaṇa Śāha to be their king. Pṛthvīnārāyaṇa sent his brother, Dalamardana Śāha, instead. Dalamardana ruled Patan until 1765, when he was forced to flee because of Pṛthvīnārāyaṇa's refusal to lift his blockade. Enraged at these developments, Jayaprakāśā had several important ministers of Patan, including Kājīs Bhinkwa and Dhanavanta assassinated. Gratified with its share in Pṛthvīnārāyaṇa's conquests in and around the Valley, Bhadgaun cooperated with him from the very beginning. The Thāpās of Palanchok were from the start in league with the Gorkhalis. To make matters worse for Jayaprakāśā, his court was overrun with agents and informers of Pṛthvīnārāyaṇa Śāha.

Faced with this situation, Jayaprakāśā requested the armed assistance of the East India Company against Pṛthvīnārāyaṇa Śāha. However, the Company's troops, his last hope against the Gorkhalis, retreated from near Sindhuli in 1767 when monsoon rains, floods and malaria prevented their onward march after they had been thoroughly routed by the Gorkhalis who simply rolled rocks down on them as they tried to fight their way up the hills. One result of this encounter was that the Gorkhalis acquired a number of 'modern' weapons abandoned by the retreating seypoys.

On 26th September 1768, Jayaprakāśā fled the palace when he belatedly found out that Pṛthvīnārāyaṇa's take-over was imminent. He tried to organise resistance against Pṛthvīnārāyaṇa Śāha from Patan. After Patan surrendered to the Gorkhalis in November of 1768, he made his way to Bhadgaun with King Tejanarasiṃha Malla of Patan. Jayaprakāśā finally aroused the patriotic feelings of the Kathmandu Valley as a whole and compelled even the mild and complacent King Ranajita Malla of Bhadgaun to stage a last ditch fight against the Gorkhalis in 1769. Jayaprakāśā bravely met his death from injuries he received in the last battle.

Jayaprakāśā Malla was called upon to meet not only the challenge of Pṛthvīnārāyaṇa but also that of adverse circumstances. Admittedly, he was impulsive by nature, but if we see his personality against the background of the treachery of his officers, the active assistance they received from Bhadgaun and Patan, and the organised attack of Pṛthvīnārāyaṇa, he appears to be a remarkable man. Jayaprakāśā's long rule in Kathmandu was a constant struggle with internal as well as external enemies. Even the prospect of a fight on a double front, rendered all the more grim by internecine disputes, did not daunt him. To his last hour, he faced the situation with fortitude and equanimity, and tried his best to meet it with all his strength and intelligence. Although his patriotism may appear parochial, from the modern point of view, it was nonetheless real.

NOTES

1. Mahesh and Dinesh Raj Pant, 'Nepālkhalḍomā Pālpālī Rājā Mukunda Senko Hamalā,' *Pūrṇimā* 45:7.
2. Deviprasad Lamsal, ed., *Bhāṣā Vaṃśāvalī*, Kathmandu, 2033 V.S., p. 101.
3. Shankar Man Rajvamsi, 'Mahindrasiṃha (Bhaskara Mallako Tāmrapatra ra Thyasko Aitihāsik Vyakhyā', *Pūrṇimā* 11:55-60. See also Mohan Prasad Khanal, 'Rājā Bhāskara Malla (Mahindra Siṃha) kā Viṣyamā Samśodhan ra Nirṇaya', *Ancient Nepal* 9 (Oct. 1969): 47-52.

CHAPTER IX

THE KINGDOM OF PATAN (c.1536-1768)

Patan, which was also sometimes called Lalitpur or Lalitapattana ('Beautiful City'), had probably been the capital of Nepal during much of the medieval period. It had accumulated a wealth of art, architecture and sculpture during the Licchavi, Thakuri and early Malla periods. Early on though, the Malla kings lost effective control of the city of Patan. There were seven feudatory families in Patan, referred to in earlier sources as the *Pradhānāṅgas* or the *mahāpātras* and in the later inscriptions as the *pramāṇas*. As early as A.D. 1383, in the reign of Ananta Malla, we find two of these feudatories, Anantapāla Varman and Ujotpāla Varman, administering Patan. They recognized the sovereignty of the Malla king, but were strong enough to maintain effective control of the city.[1]

The kings who followed Ananta Malla were weak, and there was political confusion throughout the Valley. During this period of confusion the *pramāṇas* strengthened their position. Political stability returned with the reign of Jayasthiti Malla. Though Patan was the first of the cities to recognize Jayasthiti and gave him the full royal titles, throughout his reign Patan continued to be controlled by three of the *pramāṇas* from these seven feudatory families. The situation remained the same right through the reign of Yakṣa Malla. There is evidence to show that King Ratna Malla (A.D. 1482-1520), along with his brothers Rāma Malla and Ari Malla, exercised some authority in Patan before Ratna Malla became sole king of Kathmandu. Less than a decade after Ratna Malla's death, though, (certainly by 1536) Patan had become autonomous under the leadership of Viṣṇusiṃha, one of the *pramāṇas*. Jayasiṃha and his son Kīrtisiṃha are mentioned as Viṣṇusiṃha's ancestors. Kuṣumasiṃha, son of Kīrtisiṃha, married one Jayalakṣmī, who was a *vaiśya* or a member of the trading class. Out of this union was born Viṣṇusiṃha. It is interesting to find Viṣṇusiṃha emphasizing his mother's vaiśya origin at a time when other rulers were desirous of linking their ancestry with some illustrious *kṣatriya* lineage or personage. Jayasiṃha, Viṣṇusiṃha's father, was a member of one of the leading feudal families responsible for the administration of Patan.

Viṣṇusiṃha lived until A.D. 1556 when he was succeeded by his three sons: Narasiṃha, Purandarasiṃha and Uddhavasiṃha who ruled jointly until at least 1572. By 1582 Purandarasiṃha had become sole ruler of Patan. Though Viṣṇusiṃha referred to himself merely as *mahāpātra*, and in an inscription of 1551 his sons use this title plus 'Feudal Overlord of Patan' (*maṇigalādhipati*) for him, the sons adopted the royal title of *mahārājadhirāja*. Yet they could not retain their supremacy for long. Viṣṇusiṃha's son, Purandarasiṃha, was defeated by Śivasiṃha Malla of Kathmandu, and Patan was incorporated into the state of Kathmandu. As the last available document of Purandarasiṃha is dated A.D. 1596 and the first reference to Śivasiṃha as king of Patan is dated A.D. 1599, the conquest must have taken place between 1596 and 1599.

Śivasiṃha Malla appointed his son, Hariharasiṃha as Governor of Patan in his name. After the death of Hariharasiṃha, Śivasiṃha assumed administration of Patan himself. When Śivasiṃha died in 1617 he was succeeded in Kathmandu by his elder son Lakṣmīnarasiṃha; and his younger son Siddhinarasiṃha assumed the administration of Patan. In A.D. 1620 the two brothers concluded a treaty of friendship and cooperation which clearly shows that by this time Kathmandu and Patan were separate kingdoms.

Siddhinarasiṃha (c.1618-1661) was the son of Hariharasiṃha Malla by his younger wife, Lālamatīdevī. He ascended the throne as a minor and his mother acted as his Regent. He maintained amicable relations with his brother Lakṣmīnarasiṃha, king of Kathmandu. Relations between the two states became strained only when Lakṣmīnarasiṃha's son and heir, Prātapa Malla (A.D. 1641-1674), became king of Kathmandu. Unlike his father, Prātapa Malla was not reconciled to the partition of the kingdom of Kathmandu. He caused constant pin pricks to Patan by capturing its border forts. This aggressive policy was curbed only because Kathmandu needed Patan's support against Bhadgaun.

Siddhinarasiṃha Malla was on excellent terms with the King of Gorkha, Rāma Śāha. The kings pledged not only friendship and fraternity to each other but also agreed to have a joint successor should one of them die without a male heir. Siddhinarasiṃha must have maintained friendship with the rulers of the Indian plains and the Nepal tarai also. His wife, Bhānumatī, came from the plains, and his daughter, Bhīmalakṣmī, settled there after her marriage.

Siddhinarasiṃha Malla was a man of religious disposition. He lived an austere and abstemious life, though he too had a liberal outlook on religion. He was as much devoted to the gods and goddesses of Shaivism and Vaishnavism as to the manifold deities of the Buddhist Vajrayana cult. He constructed the famous temple of Krishna in front of the Royal Palace at Lalitpur in A.D. 1636. Like the other Malla kings he too was a votary of Taleju. He regularly practised charity and performed ritualistic fire-ceremonies called *kotyāhuti*. He was also interested in dance and drama and initiated the Kartika dance-drama sequence depicting the events of the *Rāmāyaṇa*. He wrote devotional songs in Maithili called *Bhanitas Nṛsiṃha* and *Nṛpasiṃha*. He also wrote a dance drama in mixed Bengali and Maithili called *Hariścandranṛtyam* which was staged in 1651.

Siddhinarasiṃha's son, Śrīnivāsa, was born in A.D. 1627 and as soon as the boy approached adolescence his father involved him in the administration of the state. This seems to have been partly a scheme to train the boy for the tasks of ruling and partly the result of a desire to withdraw gradually from the business of government to devote himself to religious exercises. Already by 1641 Śrīnivāsa was sharing administrative responsibilities with his father. By 1649 he is listed as joint ruler with his father. In 1652 Siddhinarasiṃha set off on a two-year pilgrimage to India. In 1658 an agreement with King Prātapa Malla of Kathmandu was signed in the name of Śrīnivāsa Malla. Siddhinarasiṃha finally abdicated to go and spend his remaining days in religious retirement. Most probably this took place in 1661, the date of a medal of Śrīnivāsa which may commemorate his coronation. The date of Siddhiarasiṃha's death is not known, but his name appears again on an inscription of 1676, so it was some time after that date.

Upon the death of his Chief Minister, Viśvarāma Bhāro, Śrīnivāsa Malla appointed one Kīrtisiṃha Rājkulabhājū Chautāra to this post. However, his best known Chief Minister was a man known as Bhagiratha Bhaiyā who served him loyally. Śrīnivāsa himself referred to him as his alter ego; 'There is no difference between him and me', he said; and in fact all edicts and inscriptions bear the names of both men. We have no information on who Bhagiratha was or where he came from. From the references it is clear that he was not a member of the royal family or of the nobility. Certainly he was not from the seven noble families of Patan and he may well have been an outsider.

Śrīnivāsa Malla's kingdom touched the boundaries of Gorkha and Tanahũ in the west and Gajuripeda in the north-west. It included Dhunibesi and the adjoining areas beyond Lamidanda. In 1658, King Jagatprakāśā Malla (A.D. 1647-72) of Bhadgaun captured a military outpost on the Kathmandu-Bhadgaun frontier. This incident began a war which ended four years later in 1662 when peace was restored through Patan's mediation. However, the success of Patan's mediatory role led Kathmandu to abrogate its agreement of peace and friendship with that kingdom. It was now Bhadgaun's turn to side with Patan against Kathmandu. In 1672 Patan and Bhadgaun jointly attacked Kathmandu but were immediately repulsed by Prātapa Malla.

In 1671 Patan led a military expedition to the tarai single-handedly. A military commander, Jaga Bania, captured Śubhasiṃha, son of Rājā Harihara Sena of Morang. Between 1672 and 1675 there was regular war between Makwanpur and a coalition of the forces of Patan, Bhadgaun, Gorkha and Tanahũ forged by Śrīnivāsa Malla to meet the challenge. Morang also sided with Patan in the latter's war with Makwanpur, notwithstanding the fact that Morang and Makwanpur were ruled by the same branch of the Sena family. Their combined action against Makwanpur resulted in small territorial gains for both Patan and Bhadgaun.

After the death of King Prātapa Malla of Kathmandu in 1674 Śrīnivāsa Malla became the leading figure in the Kathmandu Valley. His influence was greatest in Kathmandu where he forced the accession of Nṛpendra Malla (the elder son of Prātapa) instead of Mahipatīndra whom Prātapa Malla had designated as his successor. He was able to seat and unseat ministers in Kathmandu at will. He arranged the return to Kathmandu of the famous courtier called Cikutī, who had been forced to flee to Patan in the time of King Prātapa Malla, and made him a high ranking official. His influence also extended to Bhadgaun whose king was also a minor, and finally he began to call himself 'The Lord of Nepal' (*nepāleśvara*).

Like his father, Siddhinarasiṃha Malla, Śrīnivāsa Malla made a large number of religious endowments. Although a devotee of Shiva, he bestowed generous land-grants on the temple of Bunga-dya (Matsyendranatha). With his wife, Mṛgavatī, he set up an image of his tutelary goddess, Taleju, in the main quadrangle of the palace.

Śrīnivāsa Malla was also fond of literature, dance and drama. He wrote a seven-act play called 'The drama of the Killing of Kaṃsa' (*Kaṃsabadhanātakam*) and vigorously carried on the tradition of the Kartik dance-drama sequence introduced by his father. He promulgated rules for the conduct of religious and social rites, especially for mourning and purification, and, according to one of the later chronicles, he made new arrangements for all of the Buddhist foundations in his territory which have remained in force until the present time.

Śrīnivāsa's son Yoganarendra was born in A.D. 1667 and like his father before him, was brought into the administration at an early age. In this case, though, it was not so much the father's doing as the son's impatience and intrigue. He began to spend money independently and to play off the *pramāṇas* against his father's advisors, especially against Bhagiratha Bhaiyā whom he resented. Eventually he was disgraced by his liaisons with low women and by engaging in a partnership with a common merchant. Disgraced by the public scandal of his son's life, Śrīnivāsa Malla's mood of despondency deepened when he lost his mother in 1679 and one of his wives two years later. The frequent breakdown of the Matsyendranath Chariot at the time of the festival, bode ill for the future to Śrīnivāsa's mind. All this led Śrīnivāsa to abdicate the throne in disgust to save the kingdom from further intrigue. Yoganarendra was crowned in December 1685. The transfer of power was smooth and peaceful, as had been the case twenty-four years earlier, when Siddhinarasiṃha made over the kingdom to his son Śrīnivāsa Malla. Śrīnivāsa Malla continued to play a mediatory role among the three kingdoms whenever necessary until his death in 1687.

Yoganarendra Malla (1685-1705) was eighteen when he became king and one of his first acts was to get rid of Bhagiratha Bhaiyā. He concocted a charge against Bhagiratha Bhaiyā which turned the populace against him and forced him to resign. Shortly after this he was murdered. Yoganarendra then appointed as his Chief Minister one Vaṃsidhara, a brother of his favourite mistress and a member of one of the seven families who had so long controlled Patan in the past.

After Lakṣmīnārāyana Jośī, Minister of the Kathmandu court, acquired a dominant position in the affairs of the whole of the Kathmandu Valley, Patan temporarily sided with Kathmandu against Bhadgaun. The king of Bhadgaun, Jagatprakāśā Malla (A.D. 1647-72), stubbornly resisted Lakṣmīnarayana's pressure by refusing to dismiss his minister Bhagirāma. Patan strengthened Kathmandu's blockade of Bhadgaun until Bhagirāma fell a victim to popular disaffection in Bhadgaun itself. By 1689 Patan had changed sides and joined Bhadgaun in attacking Kathmandu. However, in 1690 Patan waged a war of its own against both Bhadgaun and Kathmandu. Lakṣmīnarayana Jośī was assassinated in 1690, and the Kathmandu Valley then saw a brief spell of peace.

Gaja Lakṣhmi Chyasal-Tol, Patan,
1st Century B.C.

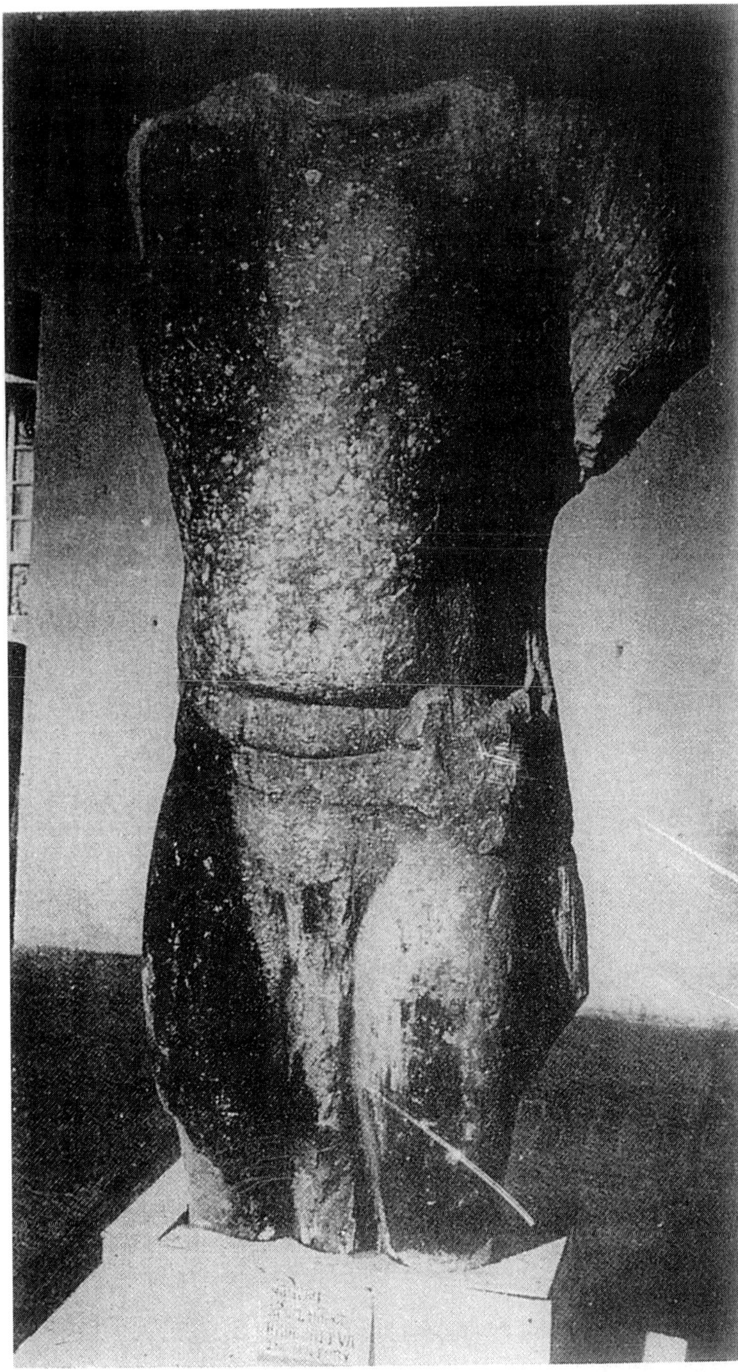

Yakṣha, National Museum, Kathmandu,
1st Century A.D.

Vaiṣṇavī Kirtipur, 2nd Century A.D.

Solar Divinity, Pashupatinath,
3rd Century A.D.

Royal Personage, National Museum, 3rd-4th Century A.D.

Viṣnu Vikrānta, Tilganga, A.D. 467

Standing Buddha, Nagal Tol, Kathmandu,
5th Century A.D.

Bodhiṣattva, Padmapāni, Ganabahal,
A.D. 550

Brahma, Chapagaun, 6th Century A.D.

Garudasana Viṣṇu, Changunarayan, 7th Century A.D.

Garuḍa, Changunarayan, 7th Century A.D.

Śiva Vishalnagar, 8th Century A.D.

Umā - Maheśvara, Kumbheshwar Dhara, Patan,
8th Century A.D.

Harihara, Narayan Chaur, 12th Century A.D.

The Bhadgaun (Bhaktapur) Darbar Square with the Fifty-five Window quadrangle

Patan (Lalitpur) Darbar Square

The Taleju temple in Kathmandu

Raja Jaya Sthitirāja Malla (1382-1395 A.D.)

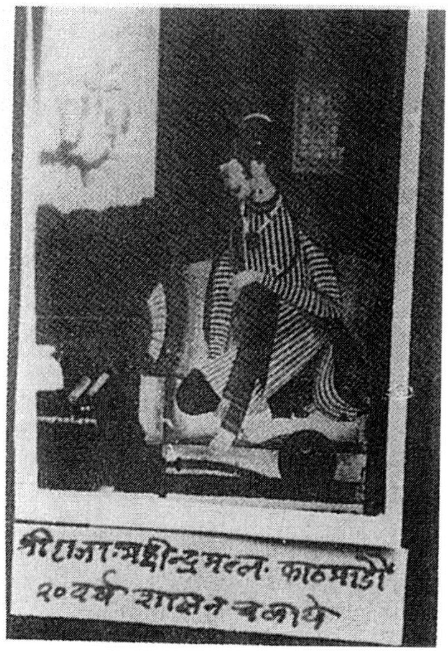

Raja Mahendra Malla (A.D. 1560-1574) of Kathmandu

Raja Pratapa Malla (A.D. 1641-1674) of Kathmandu

Raja Pārthivendra Malla (A.D. 1680-1687) of Kathmandu

Raja Siddhinarasimha Malla of Patan (c. 1618-1661)

Raja Bhupatindra Malla (A.D. 1696-1722) of Bhadgaun (Bhaktapur)

Raja Bhāskara Malla (A.D. 1700-1722) of Kathmandu

Raja Jayaprakāśa Malla (A.D. 1735-1768) of Kathmandu

In 1692 King Yoganarendra Malla raided Makwanpur in collusion with Kathmandu and Bhadgaun. This alliance did not last long, however, for Bhadgaun and Kathmandu soon forged an alliance against Patan in 1696. Then, when the King of Kathmandu was away on an elephant-catching expedition in the tarai, Patan won over Bhadgaun to its side and went into action against Kathmandu.

In 1697, the rulers of the three kingdoms of the Valley, Yoganarendra Malla of Patan, Bhūpālendra Malla of Kathmandu, and Bhūpatīndra Malla of Bhadgaun had made a joint proclamation banning every kind of contact with the members of the Ojhā family—Mahādeva, Kantu, Śyāma, Guni and Gaṅgadhara—and holding them responsible for the perpetual state of strife and dissension in the Kathmandu Valley.[2] The immediate charge against the Ojhā family was that of plotting against the life of King Bhūpālendra of Kathmandu with a view to driving a wedge between Patan and Kathmandu. But the members of the Ojhā family were then blamed for everything that had gone wrong in the Kathmandu Valley since Prātapa Malla's death in 1674. Whatever may have been the role of the Ojhās in the politics of the Kathmandu Valley, the proclamation of the kings was only an attempt to find scapegoats for their sins and those of their fathers.

Yoganarendra Malla loved poetry and music and assumed high-sounding titles such as 'Proficient in All Branches of Learning', and 'Well-versed in Dance, Art, and Music'. He also boasted of his skill in the practice of the art of eroticism or *kāmakala*. He was a man of loose sexual morals and given to profligacy. He was devoted to the goddesses Taleju and Harisiddhi, but also worshipped Lokanātha Bodhisattva Avalokiteśvara (Matsyendranath), the Buddhist deity. He also performed Hindu religious ceremonies.

Yoganarendra Malla died in 1705 at the age of 38 having been poisoned, evidently by the people of Bhadgaun whose fort of Wabhu he had under siege. Despite his numerous wives, Yoganarendra died without a legitimate male heir to succeed him. He was succeeded by his daughter Yogamatī's infant son Lokaprakāśā, and Yogamatī then came to play a prominent role in Patan politics. Lokaprakāśā ruled for only about eleven months when he died of smallpox. He was succeeded by Indra Malla (1706-1709), a son of Yoganarendra Malla's elder sister Maṇimatī and her husband Buddha Malla. The name of Indra Malla's wife, Bhāgyavatī, appears on the reverse of his coin.

Indra Malla ruled only three years dying in 1709. On the day after his death Mahindra Malla (1709-1715), an illegitimate son of Yoganarendra Malla was crowned. He had been born and raised in

Tanahū where his mother, Rājyeśvarīdevī, had gone to have her child shortly before the death of Yoganarendra. He returned to Patan with his mother, who acted as regent, but had a short reign of only about five years when he too died of smallpox. At this point, though, our sources lead to confusion. There is a coin dated 1709 bearing the name of one King Vīranarasiṃha, and a land deed of the same year which refers to King Vīranarasiṃha. A contemporary account sheds some light on the confusion. With the death of Indra Malla there was a struggle for power between Yogamatī and Rājeśvarīdevī. Yogamatī and her faction tried to set up Vīranarasiṃha as the king and issued coins in his name. We know nothing about this man except that he was a protege of Yogamatī. The theory that he was her husband needs to be further substantiated.[3] Thus for a time there may have been two rival claimants to the throne, but Vīranarasiṃha certainly lost out soon. His name appears again on a land document of A.D. 1715 but in this document Ṛddhinarasiṃha is listed as the King and Vīranarasiṃha is referred to, without royal title, as a witness to the document.

Hṛdhinarasiṃha (or Ṛddhinarasiṃha) (1715-1717) was the next king of Patan. He was the son of one Rudra Malla and grandson of Rudramatī, Śrīnivāsa Malla's daughter and Yoganarendra Malla's sister. He died two years later in 1717. At his death there was no legitimate heir and a plan was hatched to bring a king from one of the other two kingdoms. Finally, Mahendrasiṃha, king of Kathmandu, was made the king of both Kathmandu and Patan with the help of Yoganarendra's influential daughter, Yogamatī, even though Patan's ministers favoured Raṇajita Malla who was then the heir apparent of Bhadgaun. In 1719 Bhūpatīndra Malla, King of Bhadgaun (1696-1722), attacked Patan but suffered a costly defeat because his son, Raṇajita Malla, was captured by the enemy. Raṇajita was freed only on payment of a ransom of Rs. 14,000.00 and two elephants.

Mahendrasiṃha ruled Patan until his death, most probably in 1722. He was succeeded by Yogaprakāśā Malla (1722-1729). We do not know who Yogaprakāśā Malla was and how he gained the throne. Like Vīranarasiṃha Malla, he was probably a distant relative of the ruling Malla family or a protege of Yogamatī Devī. He proved to be a weak and ineffective ruler. King Raṇajita Malla of Bhadgaun bribed Jagajjaya Malla of Kathmandu to join him in a military campaign against Patan. Jagajjaya took the bribe but then linked forces with Gorkha against Bhadgaun and succeeded in extorting from Bhadgaun a ransom of two elephants and Rs. 24,000.00.

As Yogaprakāśā Malla died childless, Viṣṇu Malla (1729-1745), son of King Indra Malla's sister Punyamatī and one Darasiṃha, ascended the throne of Patan. Viṣṇu Malla's mother, Punyamatī, was a daughter of Śrīnivāsa Malla's daughter, Maṇimatī. He strengthened his political position by marrying Candralakṣmī, daughter of King Jagajjaya Malla of Kathmandu. Viṣṇu Malla and Jagajjaya Malla, with the support of Gorkha, attacked Bhadgaun in 1730 and wrested Nala and Sanga from Raṇajita Malla who later recovered those places with the help of Tanahū. Meanwhile, Gorkha, Tanahū and Lamjung started intervening in the politics of the Kathmandu Valley. Gorkha's active interest in developments inside the Valley disturbed both Lamjung and Tanahū. Viṣṇu Malla performed acts of religious piety, built temples and endowed them with land. In 1734 he reconstructed the royal palace of Patan.

As Viṣṇu Malla had no child of his own, he adopted his wife's brother, Rājyaprakāśā Malla, as his heir apparent. At Viṣṇu Malla's death in 1745 Rājyaprakāśā became king and ruled for thirteen years. His was an eventful reign. The court officials of Patan and Kathmandu entered into conspiracies together to the detriment of their supposed masters. These courtiers, so adept at underhand dealings, proved ineffective in meeting the new challenge posed by Gorkha. During the reign of Rājyaprakāśā Malla and for eight years after his death the *pramāṇas* were once more securely entrenched in their position. Little did they think that they would also be dislodged in due course.

Pṛthvinārāyaṇa Śāha of Gorkha proved more than a match for these courtiers in the art of intrigue. In a clever move to widen the gulf between Patan and Kathmandu, he wrested Lamidanda from Tanahū on Patan's behalf. The courtiers of Patan were naturally pleased with him. But subsequently Pṛthvinārāyaṇa kept Lamidanda for himself on the understanding that the people of Patan would be permitted to collect firewood and fodder from the forests of Lamidanda.

Rājyaprakāśā Malla, already helpless against the powerful officials of his court, became blind in 1752. Possibly the courtiers had a hand in blinding him. Before he died in 1758, Dahachok, Thankot, Balambu, Satingal and Pharping had already fallen into Pṛthvinārāyaṇa's hands. The courtiers of Patan then put Viśvajīta Malla on the throne. He was, according to a chronicle, the son of Viṣṇu Malla's sister, though probably his own family did not have any standing since the ancestry of Viśvajīta Malla is unclear. He was only eighteen years old when he became king and he reigned for only two years and nine months. He was assassinated by a minister's son with whose wife he was living.

After the assassination of Viśvajīta Malla in 1760, the courtiers of Patan invited King Jayaprakāśā Malla of Kathmandu to become king of Patan, but they found Jayaprakāśā too clever and energetic for them. They therefore replaced him in less than a year's time by King Raṇajita Malla of Bhadgaun. Raṇajita Malla remained King of Patan for hardly a year and half when the *pramāṇas* once again invited Jayaprakāśā Malla to be their king. This lasted for less than six months. Later, Jayaprakāśā put Kajis Dhanavanta and Bhinkwa of Patan to death after Pṛthvinārāyaṇa attacked Kīrtipur. In 1764 the *pramāṇas* invited Pṛthvinārāyaṇa himself to be King of Patan, but he sent his brother, Dalamardana Śāha, instead. Before the year 1765 had passed, Dalamardana was thrown out by the *pramāṇas* because Pṛthvinārāyaṇa refused to lift his economic blockade of Patan. In April-May of 1765 Tejanarasiṃha Malla was placed on the throne of Patan. He was the last Malla king of Patan, for Patan was conquered by Pṛthvinārāyaṇa Śāha in October of 1768 after which Tejanarasiṃha Malla fled with Jayaprakāśā of Kathmandu to Bhadgaun where the combined forces of the three kings were defeated in November of the following year by Pṛthvinārāyaṇa Śāha.

NOTES

1. Much of the history of Patan has been carried by the following four articles: Dhanavajra Vajracarya, 'Cautāā Bhagirata Bhaiyā', *Pūrṇimā* 5:21-31; 'Yoga-narendra Mallako Rajyabhiṣek', *Pūrṇimā* 9:17-22; Sankar Man Rajvami 'Yognarendra Mallakā Uttarā-dhikārī', *Pūrṇimā* 6:37-44, 'Siddhinarasiṃha Mallabhandā Agāḍikā Patsankā Śāsakharūkā Kehī Tāḍspataa', Pūrṇima 12:17-22.
2. See the section on the Kingdom of Kathmandu.
3. An inscription of N.S. 820 (A.D. 1700) which lists a number of donors and their genealogy notes one Vīrasiṃha who is the son of a daughter (Bhīmlakṣmi) of Siddhinarasiṃha. He may be the same as Viranarasiṃha. See Hem Raj Sakya and Tulsi Ram Vaidya, *Medieval Nepal*, Colophons and Inscriptions, Kathmandu, 1970, pp., xxii, 187-88.

CHAPTER X

THE KINGDOM OF BHADGAUN (C. 1496-1769)

After the partition of the Kathmandu Valley among Yakṣa Malla's sons, the kingdom of Bhadgaun consisted of Changu, Sanga, Nakades, Thimi and Bode as well as the town of Bhadgaun itself. By 1496 Rāya Malla was the sole ruler of Bhadgaun. At his death in 1505 he was succeeded by his son Bhuvana Malla, a minor. Raṇa Malla, who then ruled the separate kingdom of Banepa, returned to Bhadgaun to assist his nephew. When he died childless Banepa was reabsorbed by Bhadgaun.

Bhuvana Malla's rule was followed by the joint rule of Jīta Malla and Prāṇa Malla (1518-c.1545). However, from 1534 Prāṇa Malla ruled alone. Nothing definite can be said about the relationship between Jīta Malla and Prāṇa Malla. There is not a single document of the period in which Jīta Malla figures alone, whereas there are at least ten documents that mention Prāṇa Malla alone. This has led some writers to infer that Jīta Malla may have been Prāṇa Malla's younger brother, and that he was mentioned only out of courtesy along with his elder brother, the *de facto* and *de jure* ruler. However, whenever both names occur, Jīta Malla is mentioned first. The precedence given to Jīta Malla in this way has led one author to conclude that he may have been an uncle of Prāṇa Malla.

Prāṇa Malla's son and successor, Viśva Malla (c.1545-1559), and his queen, Gaṅgā Rāni, were noted for their religious deeds. Viśva Malla made additions and repairs to the temple of Dattatreya and also set up a monastery for Shaiva ascetics. Viśva Malla was succeeded by his son, Trailokya Malla (c. 1560-1614). Trailokya is mentioned along with his younger brother, Trivhuvana Malla, in some of his inscriptions. The dowager queen, Gaṅgā Rāni, who was running the country's administration during the reign of her son, Trailokya, probably wanted both of her sons to be mentioned in the inscriptions. But the fact that

Trailokya is mentioned as the predecessor of the Bhadgaun kings in genealogies leaves no room for doubt that he was the eldest son and the reigning monarch.

Trailokya Malla was succeeded by his son, Jagajjyotīr Malla (c.1614-1637) who was a great lover of music, poetry, drama and dance. He was conversant with the Bhatkhande school of Indian music. He initiated the Bisket festival of Bhairava, which is observed to this day in Bhadgaun. He authored a treatise on music called *Saṅgītabhaśkara* in collaboration with Vaṃsamaṇi Jhā, who also wrote for the Kathmandu Court two plays in Maithili, *Gītādigaṃvara* and *Muditamadālāsā*. Jagajjyotira Malla compiled a collection of songs in Sanskrit called *Gītapāñcasikā*. He also composed the *Dasāvatāra Nṛtya*, a religious poem. He is credited with the authorship of three dramas in Maithili, *Muditakuvalayāśva*, *Hara Gaurīvivāha*, and *Kuñjavihārinātaka*. Despite the defects in language, the last two plays, in the opinion of Sylvain Levi, approach the standard of the plays of Kalidasa and Bhavabhuti in their wealth of melody and imagery. Jagajjyotira Malla also wrote a commentary on Vatsayana's *Kāmasūtra*, the well-known Sanskrit treatise on sex.

Nareśa Malla (c.1637-1643), called Narendra Malla by later chronicles, succeeded his father Jagajjyotira. Nareśa Malla was once defeated in battle by Pratāpa Malla, King of Kathmandu. At his death in 1643 he was succeeded by his son Jagatprakāśa Malla (1643-1672), a boy of less than five years. Though it is not clear who ran the administration during his childhood two different Chief Ministers are mentioned Dhanadasiṃha and Viśva Bhāro. As a young man his Chief Minister was Candraśekhara Siṃha Bhājū. Although very little is known about Candraśekhara Siṃha's achievements, he is mentioned and highly praised by King Jagatprakāśa Malla in a number of inscriptions from this period in his life. From 1660 on Jagatprakāśa Malla suffered a series of defeats at the hands of King Pratāpa Malla of Kathmandu. After being rescued by King Śrīnivāsa Malla of Patan from a precarious situation, Jagatprakāśa acknowledged his gratitude to the Patan king in verse.

Jagatprakāśa Malla had a taste for poetry and music. He called himself 'King of Poets' (*kavīndra*) and 'Teacher and Master of Music' (*gandharvavidyaguru*). He composed a collection of poems called *Nānāraṅgagītasaṅgraha* when he was very young. His other known works are *Padyasamucchaya* and *Gītapañcaka*. He died at the age of thirty-four in the year 1672 leaving two young sons.

Jitāmitra Malla (1672-1696) succeeded his father Jagatprakāśa Malla at an early age and his Chief Minister, Bhagirāma Pradhānāṅga, was a great asset to the young king. However, Lakṣminārāyaṇa Jośī, the powerful minister at the Kathmandu Court, was jealous of Bhagirāma and pressured King Jītāmitra Malla to get rid of his trusted minister. He even subjected Bhadgaun to a blockade with a view to causing the common people to rise against the minister. The blockade served the purpose, and the people requested King Jitāmitra to dismiss his minister. When the king refused to grant their demand, they dragged Bhagirāma through the streets and forced the king to dismiss him. Śyāmadāsa Mūlamī and Hāku Bhājū became ministers after Bhagirāma. Jītāmitra was interested in the well-being of his people and during his reign, new canals were dug and measures adopted for their maintenance. Rules were also made for the use and sharing of water.

Like other rulers of Bhadgaun, Jītāmitra was a man of artistic temperament. He built annexes to the royal palace and was credited with providing four murals in the hall of the palace depicting the story of the *Rāmāyaṇa* and for having beautiful struts with images of the 'Eight Mother Goddesses' (*aṣṭamātṛka*) carved. He also wrote several literary works in Sanskrit and Maithili. *Aśwamedhanāṭakam* was one of his plays, and he also wrote a commentary on the *Gītagovindam* by Jayadeva, the well-known writer of erotic and devotional songs in Sanskrit.

Jitāmitra was essentially a man of peace and spared no pains to improve his relations with the neighbouring kingdoms of Patan and Kathmandu. On the occasion of the Harisiddhi dance and of the Scimitar Procession (*khaḍga jātrā*), frequent fights broke out among the people of Bhadgaun and Patan. Jītāmitra entered into an agreement with King Yoganarendra Malla of Patan to take every precaution to avoid these skirmishes. In disregard of this agreement, Patan joined Kathmandu in attacking Bhadgaun, but the joint attack was repulsed. Mindful of the trouble and confusion so recently caused in Patan by the profligacy and intrigue of Yoganarendra against his father Śrīnivāsa, Jitāmitra brought his son, Bhūpatīndra Malla, into the administration early and trained him for his duties. In 1696 he abdicated in favour of his son and went into retirement dying only in 1709.

Jitāmitra's son and successor, Bhūpatīndra Malla (1696-1722) was a great builder. He added new wings to the royal palace of Bhadgaun and refurnished its main courtyard with a miniature temple of Taleju Bhavānī. He had a glass pane set into one of the fifty-five windows of the palace he built. The pane of glass had been given to him by someone from India and proved to be an object of curiosity to all. He installed a bronze statue of himself in front of the palace which still stands, and he also erected an image of Ākāśa Bhairava in the palace square. He had malaticok front of the palace fitted with sandal-wood windows, which overlooked the main gateway. He also set up an image of Hanūmān, the monkey god, and Narasiṃha, the half-man half-lion god, on the pattern of imags outside the gate of Kathmandu palace.

It was duting his reign that the water conduit at Kwalakhutol and the famous five-storeyed temple, called Nyātpola in Newari, were built. This temple is an outstanding example of the Nepali pagoda. Amusing and interesting at the same are the images of two wrestlers, named after the two well known Rajput heroes of the sixteenth century—Jayamal and Patta — as doorkeepers in charge of the paved stairway lined on both sides with figures of lions, griffins, and elephants. His son and heir apparent, Raṇajita Malla, is mentioned with him as co-builder of some of the above monuments and also as a partner in the performance of charitable and religious deeds.

Bhūpatīndra Malla resembled an earlier king of Kathmandu, Pratāpa Malla (1671-74), not only in his zeal for building enterprises, but also in temperament and character. He shared Pratāpa Malla's domineering spirit and sought aggrandizement at the cost of the neighbouring kingdoms of Patan and Kathmandu. Once Bhūpatīndra was trapped when his son, Raṇjita Malla, fell into the hands of his enemies at Bisankhu on one of Bhadgaun's ferquent forays into Patan's territory. The heir apparent himself was held to ransom and was subsequently freed only when King Bhūpatīndra made payment. He had to seek peace with King Yoganarendra Malla of Patan and let the latter visit Bhadgaun to worship at the original image of Taleju, the tutelary goddess of the Malla family.

Like Pratāpa Malla, Bhūpatīndra Malla also composed poems. A collection of his poems in Maithili, called *Padyāvāli*, is highly rated by ciritics. He also worte dramas, one of them based on the *Mahābhārata*. The lament of King Dhṛtrāṣṭra, father of the Kauravas, over the loss of his one hundred sons in the Armageddon of the *Mahābhārata* is remarkable for its poignant pathos.

Bhūpatīndra Malla was able to persuade King Yoganarendra Malla of Patan to join himself and the rulers of Gorkha and Makwanpur in pledging that in case anyone of the four entered into relations with Kathmandu, without the prior knowledge of the others, the defaulter would have to pay a penalty of Rs. 40,000.00. But this did not prevent Patan from attacking Bhadgaun. During Bhūpatīndra Malla's rule

Bhadgaun was attacked four times by Patan and Kathmandu after the last two had patched up their old differences. However, it must be said to the credit of Bhūpatīndra Malla, that he successfully repulsed the combined attack of Patan and Kathmandu everytime. He had friendly relations with Makwanpur, where he took part in 'Elephant Capturing Operations' (*hātīkhedah*).

Bhūpatīndra Malla died early in 1722 and was succeeded by his son, Raṇajita Malla (1722-1769). On the frame of the golden door set up by Raṇajita Malla and his wife, Jayalakṣmī, to commemorate the performance of the religious rite of fire (*kotyāhuti*), Raṇajita is mentioned as ruler of the territory that extended to the Dudhkoshi river in the east, including the town of Dolakha.

Raṇajita Malla had a long reign of forty-seven years. He was a man of kindly disposition and of soft and amicable nature, and was thus unsuited to rule at a time of political conflict. Pṛthvinārāyaṇa Śāha, the ruler of Gorkha, exploited Raṇajita Malla's basic goodness to make him an instrument for the destruction of his own kingdom and the whole Malla dynasty.

During his stay as a guest at the court of Bhadgaun before he became king, Pṛthvinārāyaṇa had contracted a relationship of ritual brotherhood with Raṇajita Malla's eldest son, Vīranarasiṃha Malla, who died early under rather suspicious circumstances. Thus, Raṇajita Malla was Pṛthvinārāyaṇa 's ritual father. Raṇajita Malla was attached to Pṛthvinārāyaṇa because of this and also because of his temperamental abhorrence of the overbearing manners of King Jayaprakāśa Malla of Kathmandu. This attachment made him indifferent to the threat to the existence of the three kingdoms of the Kathmandu Valley posed by the gradual ascendancy of Gorkha. Neither the other two Valley rulers nor the king of Gorkha enjoyed the same prestige among the common people as Raṇajita Malla, the only direct ruling descendant of Yakṣa Malla and Jayasthiti Malla. If he had risen to the occasion and acted in time, it might have been difficult for Pṛthvinārāyaṇa to conquer the Valley. Even with all the lapses of Raṇajita and the other rulers, it took the Gorkha King twenty-seven years to accomplish the conquest of the Kathmandu Valley.

Like other kings of the valley, Raṇajita Malla had many wives and several children. His favourite mistress persuaded him to pass over the claim of his first-born and legitimate child and make her own son heir-apparent instead. Naturally, the sympathy of the ministers and the common people were with the legitimate queen, who left the palace and took up residence in the village of Thimi. She was warmly received by the local people and proclaimed their sovereign. Pressure was steadily brought to bear on the king through constant representations by several groups of people who were allowed inside the main hall of the palace in accordance with an old custom of personal audiences. Finally, King Raṇjita Malla yielded to popular pressure, and with due apology to his people, he accepted the legitimate child's right. The queen returned to the royal palace with the infant prince.

King Jayaprakāśa Malla of Kathmandu took advantages of this situation in Bhadgaun to gain control of some forts within its territory. Patan, too, capitalized on the disturbed situation in Bhadgaun and anexed a piece of Bhadgaun's territory near the tri-junction of Bhadgaun, Patan and Makwanpur. Those depredations by Kathmandu and Patan initially inclined Raṇjita Malla to support Gorkha and its king, Pṛthvinārāyaṇa.

By 1754 the Kathmandu Valley was constantly exposed to intermittent attacks by Pṛthvinārāyaṇa's troops, who had already encircled it with military outposts on the surrounding hills. With the help of Raṇjita Malla, Pṛthvinārāyaṇa captured Naldum and Mahadev Pokhari to the east of Kathmandu Valley. The Gorkhali troops were already entrenched in their outposts on the north-western ridge of Dahachok overlooking the Valley. Pṛthvinārāyaṇa made a deal with Raṇajita Malla for their joint forces to wrest Changu and Sankhu from Kathmandu. The understanding was that once these two places were seized, they would be left in the possession of Bhadgaun. Raṇajita Malla rightly sensed Pṛthvinārāyaṇa 's ulterior motive in making the deal and did not send his forces on the appointed day. The result was that Pṛthvinārāyaṇa's advancing forces were forced to retreat from Jitpur. Pṛthvinārāyaṇa himself was completely at the mercy of Raṇajita Malla, but the Bhadgaun ruler refused to surrender the Gorkha leader to King Jayaprakāśa Malla notwithstanding the Kathmandu king's earnest pleas.

Once Pṛthvinārāyaṇa was out of the area of Bhadgaun, he did not forgive Raṇajita Malla for his failure to keep his word. Pṛthvinārāyaṇa took back Kabhrepalanchok and Sindhupalchok, which the Gorkhas themselves had earlier conquered and left in possession of Bhadgaun. Pṛthvinārāyaṇa had plans for capturing Raṇajita Malla himself at Palanchok, but Raṇajita Malla escaped by virtue of a fortuitous absence from the palace. By 1757, even Raṇajita Malla had realized Gorkha's menace, and joined hands with the kings of Kathmandu and Patan in repulsing the invasion of Kirtipur. But by then it was too late.

Pṛthvinārāyaṇa had already ringed the Valley with his military outposts and had closed its gate to Tibet through the control of

Kabhrepalanchok and Sindhupalchok in the east. He also conquered Makwanpur in 1762 and repulsed an attack on it by Ali Mir Kasim's forces from India led by Gurgin Khan in 1763. With Makwanpur also under Pṛthvinārāyaṇa's control, the outlet for trade with India was blocked.

In 1764 an attack by Pṛthvinārāyaṇa on Kirtipur was again repulsed by the people of Kirtipur. This time they got no help from the other kings of the Valley who were quarrelling among themselves as they had done before. Patan had Pṛthvinārāyaṇa's brother, Dalamardana Śāha, as king for a few months in 1764-65. In 1765, Gorkha's troops attacked Kirtipur for the third time and finally took it by storm. Now the days of the Valley kingdoms were numbered. On 25th September 1768 Kathmandu fell into the hands of Pṛthvinārāyaṇa and on 6th October Patan followed suit. The displaced kings of Patan and Kathmandu took refuge at Bhadgaun and together fought a last-gasp action against the Gorkhas in 1769, but of no avail. On 10th November the Gorkhas broke through the eastern gate and poured into the city. The three kings, under the leadership of Jayaprakāśa Malla of Kathmandu, put up a valiant fight, but surrendered on the 12th after Jayaprakāśa himself was wounded in the leg by a musket ball.

Pṛthvinārāyaṇa had delayed action against Bhadgaun even after he acquired Kathmandu and Patan for two reasons. First, he needed time to consolidate his newly acquired position in Kathmandu and Patan. Second, Pṛthvinārāyaṇa did not want to appear ungrateful to his ritual father, Raṇajita Malla, as he was sure that Bhadgaun would fall into his hands in due time. But the presence of the displaced kings of Kathmandu and Patan in Bhadgaun gave Pṛthvinārāyaṇa an excuse to ask Raṇajita Malla for their surrender. When Raṇajita Malla refused to hand them over to Pṛthvinārāyaṇa, he attacked Bhadgaun and occupied it. However, Pṛthvinārāyaṇa treated Raṇajita Malla with respect even after his defeat. As Raṇajita Malla himself expressed a desire to live a retired life in Varanasi, Pṛthvinārāyaṇa allowed him to go, taking all his personal wealth with him.

CHAPTER XI

SOCIAL CONDITIONS IN MEDIEVAL NEPAL

Political Conditions

During the medieval period, as in ancient Nepal under the Licchavi dynasty, absolute monarchy by divine right was the form of government. Such royal titles as *bhagavatapaśupati bhaṭṭāraka pādanugrihita*" stated that the ruler enjoyed a special blessing at the feet of Lord Pashupati.

The other titles adopted by the ruling monarchs were 'King of Kings'(*mahārājadhirāja*) 'Great God' (*parameśvara*), 'The Most Venerable (*paramabhaṭṭaraka*), 'Overlord of Kings' (*rājadhirāja*). The later Malla rulers of the three kingdoms in the Valley styled themselves 'Lord of Nepal' (*nepāleśvara*) or 'Lord of the Whole of Nepal's Land Area' (*nepālamahimaṇḍalakhaṇḍa*). The royal titles retained the reference to the favour or blessing at Lord Pashupati's feet, and also mentioned the favour of Māneśvari, the tutelary deity of the dynasty adopted by Jayasthiti Malla and his successors (*māneśvarīṣṭadevatarcaraṇa labhdaprasāda*). The titles of the Kings of Kathmandu and Bhadgaun referred to the presence of Hanūmān or the monkey god in their standards (*hanūmāndhwaja*). But the crowning section of the title, shared in common by all the Malla Kings of the Valley, and still retained by the Shah King of Nepal is 'Lord of the Mountains, Crest Jewel of the Wheel, God Among Men' (*girirājacakracuḍāmaṇi naranārāyaṇa*).

The period between 1274 and 1382 was characterized by instability and uncertainty, as we have seen above. During this period, the Khasya Kings of the Karnali region invaded the Kathmandu Valley: Jitāri Malla in 1287, 1289, and 1290; Ripu Malla in 1312; his successor, Āditya Malla, in 1328, and Puṇya Malla in 1334. In addition to this there were repeated incursions by the Ḍoya (the Tirhutiyas from Simraungarh). However, the invasion by Sultan Shamshudin Iliyas of Bengal (1342-

1357) in 1349 proved to be the most devastating. The impact of these invasions was aggravated by the unstable situation which already prevailed in the Kathmandu Valley. Centrifugal tendencies received an impetus and several men with strong local influence appeared upon the scene.

The absence of an organized feudal hierarchy made it possible for the Kings of the Kathmandu Valley to act without any restraint. Perhaps the small size of their kingdoms was not conducive to the growth of an effective feudal organization, but whenever feudal elements did emerge, they were able to curb the absolute powers of the monarch. The roles of the Jīvas of Udayapur, of the chiefs of Dhavalasrotri, of the Rāma-Varddhanas of Banepa, of the so-called Thakuri chiefs of Nuwakot and Patan and, to a lesser extent, of the Ravutas of Pharping deserve mention in this connection.

The system of dual government (*dvairājya*) meant different things at different times. Some times it meant two kings ruling two separate territorial units which formed an integral part of one and the same kingdom, one of the kings having a subordinate position. At other times, it implied joint rule of the kingdom as a whole by two kings of equal status. Along with *dvairājya*, the word *ardharājya*, which means 'government of one-half' of the kingdom, occurs in the inscriptions and colophons of the period between 1000 and 1382.

This system of dual government was used at times by both the Thakuris and the Mallas. The dual government of Narendradeva (c. 998-999) and Udayadeva (c. 998-1004) and of Nirbhayadeva (c. 1004-1009) Rudradeva (c. 1007-1028) and Bhojadeva (c. 1009-1020) in the pre-Malla period, and the joint rule of Jayānandadeva (1361-1382) and Jayasthiti Malla may be cited as examples. After Jayasthiti Malla's death in 1395, his three sons Jayadharma Malla, Jayajyotir Malla, and Jayakīrti Malla ruled the kingdom jointly. This provided an example of three-man rule (*trayarājya*).

Sylvain Levi has quoted a quatrain from Kalidasa's drama *Malavikagnimitra* in praise of the system of *dvairājya*. The English translation of the stanza is as follows: 'These two kings, supporting the fortune of their overlord divided between them, as the horses support the yoke of their charioteer, will remain firm in their allegiances to thee, without being distracted by mutual attacks'. Despite Levi's praise of the system, the dual or the triple government, which undermined the authority of the state, may be taken as the precursor of the subsequent partition of the kingdom of the Kathmandu Valley into three kingdoms after 1482. The ideal working of the system, as visualized in Kalidasa's stanza, may have been frustrated in Nepal by the absence of a dominating paramount ruler to keep the co-rulers in their places.

The Crown Prince (*yuvarāja*) was mentioned in some inscriptions together with the other favourite sons of the ruling monarch (*mahārājakumāra*). Their actual powers depended on the nature of their relationship with their ruling fathers. After Yakṣa Malla (1428-1482), the Kathmandu Valley suffered fragmentation, with disastrous consequences for both the kingdoms and the dynasty. Pratāpa Malla's demonstrated partaility for one son gave rise to serious friction among his sons after death over the question of succession. The result was that his favourite son, Mahipatīndra Malla, was deposed and persecuted all his life by his half-brothers. As a rule, the eldest prince was regarded as the heir apparent. Whenever this rule was isolated without sufficient reason, the political consequences were disastrous.

Polygamy was common. It often led to fierce competition among the wives of the king for the status of 'the favourite wife' and to savage struggles to obtain the right of succession for their sons. Concubinage created a further problem of whether sons born out of wedlock should be allowed to succeed to the throne. Problems of succession were, as a rule, resolved smoothly and expeditiously. However, there was much controversy about legitimate and illegitimate succession during the reign of Raṇajita Malla (1722-1769), the last Malla King of Bhadgaun, who favoured an illegitimate son for succession to the throne. The controversy was resolved only by the Gorkha conquest.

Women were generally debarred from succession to the throne. However, this did not imply that women had no role in influencing political developments, or that the husbands and sons of royal women were debarred from succession. The role of Princess Nāyakadevī and her daughter, Princess Rājalladevī, of Bhadgaun, and of their grandmothers, Padumalladevī and Devaladevī, who functioned as their regents, deserves mention in this connection. Jayasthiti Malla (1382-1395), Rājalladevī's husband, founded a new dynasty which lasted 350 years. Mothers of infant rulers generally exercised considerable authority as regents during the minority of their sons. Yogamatī, daughter of King Yoganarendra Malla of Patan, played a conspicuous role as a king-maker.

Religion, in a rather narrow sense, influenced the life of the people; and astrologers and sooth-sayers were invariably consulted before political enterprises were undertaken. Even then, religion was treated merely as a hand-maid of politics. A Nepali counterpart of Cardinal Wolsey or Cardinal Richelieu never emerged. Men of religion remained advisors to the rulers without political ambitions of their own.

Feudal titles, for people of importance who were not royalty were often connected with administrative functions but became hereditary in due course. The title Sāmanta or Mahāsāmanta used in the earlier period occurs also occasionally in the early medieval period also. Among others, the ruler of Pannaga or Panumga is mentioned in 1150 and 1160 as a Mahāsāmanta, as is the feudatory chief of Udayapura (1066, 1104, 1120 and 1128). The highest office or title was that of *mahātha* (Sk. *mahattaka*) 'Prime Minister'. It was used at least once (for the heir apparent Jayadharma Malla) in 1377 as a purely honorary title for a royal prince. This title was also held by Anekarāma Varddhana and Jayasiṃharāma Varddhana of Banepa.

The most common title for the average nobleman in the medieval period was *bhāro* (or *bhāroka, bhalloka)* which one finds as early as the eleventh century. In the 14th century the term *mūlamī* came into use and soon became the title used by most of the leading nobles. Both of these titles were peculiar to the landed aristocracy. The city nobility (*pradhāna*) had different titles. In Patan the typical title for the nobility was *pātra* or *māhapātra* to which title was added *pradhānaṅga.* Eventually seven families of these *māhapātras* became the dominant families of the city and are frequently referred to as the *saptakutumbaja māhapātras*, the 'Seven Noble Families'. Eventually these families formed a sort of council which controlled the affairs of the city. Later they are referred to as the *prāmaṇas*, a title which seems to indicate 'Official Certifier' or 'Notary'. The ruling nobles of Pharping referred to themselves as *rāvuta* or *mahārāvuta* ('Principal Ancillary Chief').

The commander-in-chief was called *jodhapati* (Sk. *yuddhapati*). The military officer in charge of a garrison fort was called *kvāṭhanāyaka* (Sk. *koṣṭanāyaka*). Titles in Sanskrit such as *amātya, mantri, rājaguru,* and *dharmādhikāra* were also used at times. Little information is available about the common people. Some inscriptions mention goldsmiths as 'donors' of some religious images, but nothing is known about the merchant class.

Two or three incidents, mentioned in the chronicles and also in the accounts of contemporary Christian missionaries, indicate that the people exercised some form of control over the despotic acts of the rulers. As we have seen in the cases of King Sadāśiva Malla of Kathmandu, King Jitāmitra of Bhadgaun and his minister, the unfortunate Bhagirāma, the common people could exercise their right only in exceptional circumstances. Public opposition to the appointment of a Muslim as Chief Minister by King Mahendrasiṃha of Kathmandu and Patan forced him to cancel the appointment. When Raṇajita Malla wanted to nominate his illegitimate son as his successor, Thimi's action and popular clamour forced him to apologise to the people and drop the proposal. The reaction to the cold-blooded murder of King Viśvajīta Malla of Patan by a court-official's son, with whose wife he lived in sin, may be cited as another example of popular action against the ruler. But all these incidents were rather unusual. They do not indicate that the people had a constitutional means of effective control over the king, but they do show that the people were not docile and unconcerned with politics. Even the apparently spontaneous uprisings may have been instigated by frustrated court officials or royal relatives.

The fragmentation of the Kathmandu Valley into three separate kingdoms after the death of King Yakṣa Malla in 1482 proved to be a disaster for the Malla dynasty. The three kingdoms, although ruled by descendants of the same family and with their frontiers within a few miles of their capitals, were perpetually torn by internal dissension. The rulers' vision, over a period of three hundred and fifty years, hardly ever extended beyond the Valley and its adjoining areas such as Palanchok and Nuwakot.

The rulers of all the three kingdoms sought personal aggrandizement at the cost of each other. Whenever one of the rulers made any sort of gain, the other two would combine against him. Joint raids into Makwanpur and Morang did not result in lasting and positive gains for any one of them. The rulers sought the assistance of Gorkha as well as of Tanahũ and Lamjung whenever they were pressed by any one side in their fratricidal war. However, Gorkha, Tanahũ and Lamjung did not intervene in the affairs of the Kathmandu Valley without the prospect of real acquisitions for themselves.

It was not merely a case of mutual jealousy and rivalry among the three rulers. Court life had become charged with intrigue and suspicion at every level. Ministers conspired against ministers, sons against fathers, brothers against brothers and wives against husbands. Unscrupulous courtiers hired agents and professional assassins. Courtiers plotted among themselves, but the successful plotters were soon paid back in their own coin. The ladies of the royal household, and even regent queens, became subjects of court scandals. Powerful ministers of the Malla court, such as Cikutī, Bhagirāma and Lakṣmīnārāyaṇa Jośi gained power as a result of conspiracies during the minority of the rulers. However, they did not wield power for long and soon fell a prey to counter-plots.

In 1696 a joint proclamation of the three kings of the Valley, Bhūpālendra Malla of Kathmandu, Bhūpatīndra Malla of Bhadgaun and

Yoganarendra Malla of Patan, condemned and banned the members of the Ojhā family as arch-criminals and conspirators, and warned the public against having anything to do with them. As a lasting monument to the hypocrisy and self-deception of these decadent rulers, there exists to this day in the main quadrangle (Mulchok) of the old Patan palace a copperplate on which their joint proclamation is inscribed. The statement itself is poignant with a deep sense of pathos and irony, and reflects a measure of self-pity and self-condemnation on the part of those who were a party to it. In this joint proclamation the rulers seek to blame the Ojhās for the faults of their Malla fathers and themselves. But to posterity their efforts appear merely as a wilful design to divert the attention of the common people from the sordid and sinister reality of contemporary court life and politics. The rulers conveniently forgot, and wanted the people to forget too, that those fallen arch-criminals and villains were, in fact, the creations and instruments of the sinister will of the highly placed victims themselves.

Thanks to the natural defenses of the Kathmandu Valley, its fertile soil, its favourable location for trade and, above all, to the constructive attitude and industry of its common people, the three kingdoms of the Kathmandu Valley, despite their endless political intrigues and chronic instability, endured for a period of 350 years without experiencing internal revolution or external conquest.

In spite of all the pomp and glitter of the royal courts, and in spite of their interest in art, culture and literature, the later Malla rulers proved politically ineffective. The main fabric of their political life had worn out, and became thin and thread-bare. Perpetual conspiracy, fraud and deceit had undermined their moral fibre; and their health and character were equally affected by their excesses.

Economic and Social Conditions

Set against the extravagance and degradation of the court life, the solid and lasting achievements of the common people in the field of agriculture and trade, as well as art, architecture and sculpture appear surprising. It is possible to admire innumerable buildings and statues; lovely additions to palaces and temples with artistic windows and doors, that are in themselves fine specimens of wood carving and trellis work; tastefully decorated water conduits and fountains of the finest design and quality; elegant and neatly laid out squares in front of the royal palaces; and quadrangles of palaces decorated with finely wrought images of gods and goddesses by Newari artists, artisans and ordinary labourers over a period of centuries.

The fertile soil of the Kathmandu Valley and the industry and skill of its people in agriculture and trade provided not only for basic needs, but also for frequent religious and social festivals and chariot processions (*jātrās*). Documentary evidence regarding specific economic conditions of Nepal during the medieval period exists, but so far scholars have not studied these in depth. However, we know that the people in the Kathmandu Valley were a prosperous agricultural community. A section of its enterprising members were very successful in trade. Some of the more prosperous merchants were engaged in the profitable entrepot trade between Tibet and India through Nepal. The position of the Kathmandu Valley as a main centre for entrepot trade in the trans-Himalayan region imparted economic vitality to a society which had few viable alternatives open to it. During the Malla period, the Kathmandu Valley as a main centre for entrepot trade in the trans-Himalayan region imparted economic vitality to a society which had few viable alternatives open to it. During the Malla period, the Kathmandu Valley owed its prosperity largely to this trade. The Malla rulers ahd drawn much of their revenue from direct participation in the complicated trading system which linked the East India Company and Tibet through Newari traders, Gosains, and Kashmiri Muslim Trading houses.

Nepal's parctice of minting coins for Tibet was also an additional source of profit to the Malla rulers of the Kathmandu Valley. Apart from charging a handsome fee for minting coins, the Malla rulers also exploited the frequent fluctuations in the price of bullion on the Indian market and used to their own advantage the exchange rate of gold and silver for rupees, which was fixed with Tibet on an annual basis. However, Rājā Raṇajita Malla of Bhadgaun and Rājā Jayaprakāśa Malla of Kathmandu taxed to the utmost this profitable system of minting coins for Tibet in order to ensure the supply of funds they needed for their internecine disputes and for their war against the Gorkhas. In the process, both monarchs seriously debased the value of the coins minted by reducing the ratio of silver to other less valuable metals. This increased the revenue for the Malla Kings concerned but it seriously undermined the confidence of Tibetans in the Nepali currency. The result was a long-standing dispute after the Gorkha conquest of the Kathmandu Valley over the circulation of Nepali currency in Tibet, with adverse consequences to the India-Nepal-Tibet trading system.

Coinage is the only category of economic history about which bits of information can be pieced together. The period of the Licchavis and their successors yields coins which, though undated, correspond to the inscriptions of the period in Gupta characters. Although literary evidence shows that in the 12th century Śivadeva struck gold and silver coins, these have not yet been discovered. Mahendra Malla (1564-1574), King of Kathmandu, minted silver coins which mentioned the name of his kingdom, 'Kāṣṭhamaṇḍapa' along with his name. No Nepali coins of the period between the 8th and the 16th centuries are available.

Gold coins seem to have disappeared quite early from circulation. After Mahendra Malla remodelled the currency in the 16th century, only silver coins remained in circulation. Silver coins minted in Nepal were legal tender in Tibet for a long time before Gorkha conquest of the Valley in 1768-69.

A system of standard weights and measures prevailed in medieval Nepal. Land was measured in terms of *javas* and *ropanīs*, four *javas* making one *ropanī* which was equivalent to 343.6 square feet. The standard volume measures were *mānā*, *pāthī* and *murī*. One *mānā* was equivalent to one pint. Eight *mānās* made one *pāthī* and twenty *pāthīs* made one *murī*. The prevalence of a system of standard currency, weights and measures shows that the Kathmandu Valley's economy was fairly well developed during the medieval period. Although a market economy in the modern sense did not exist, there were several trade centres where buyers and sellers would gather on certain fixed days.

The system of private and public trusts called '*gūṭhī*' was a remarkable feature of Nepali social and economic life during the medieval period. Their elaborate organization, on the basis of occupational castes, suggests a comparison with the guild system in medieval Europe. But the *gūṭhīs* were, in fact, more comprehensive than the guilds in their scope and regulated not only the profession or occupation but also the social and religious life of their members. The caste-system, as regulated by Jayasthiti Malla in Nepal, proceeded immediately to a scheme of sixty-four occupational sub-castes, without bothering about the classical four *varṇas*, or castes, which had only a marginal bearing on the prevailing conditions in Nepal. The system of the sixty-four occupational castes such as *chitrakāra* (painters), *takṣakāra* (carpenters), *śilpakāra* (craftsmen) etc., each with a guild or gūṭhī of its own to regulate not only its economic but also social and religious life, indicates a fairly advanced level of economic and social activity with a large variety of specialized functions performed by a number of occupational castes.

CHAPTER XII

RELIGION IN MEDIEVAL NEPAL

The broad and pragmatic outlook of the people on religious matters helped the growth and synthesis of different religious sects and beliefs on an eclectic basis.

It is not known precisely when Buddhism actually entered the Kathmandu Valley, but there can be no doubt that it did so from the south. Buddhism is said to have been introduced into Nepal either by Gautama Buddha himself or by Emperor Aśoka and his daughter. However, little is known about its history except for the Ashokan pillars at Niglihava and Rupandehi in the Kapilavastu district of the Lumbini Zone, and the *stūpas* at Patan in the Kathmandu Valley.

While Buddhism was still engaged in its steady and continuing struggle with shamanism, or primitive animism, in and across the Himalaya, Brahmanism in the Indian plains was gradually re-establishing its age-old authority against the comparatively new doctrine of Buddhism. But it was not until the eleventh century that the Buddhists finally gave up their struggle in India. Thereafter, they either conformed to Hinduism or sought sanctuary in Nepal, Bhutan and Sikkim. Even in the Kathmandu Valley and elsewhere in the hill regions of Nepal Buddhism had to concede a good deal to Brahmanic tradition, just as it had to make large concessions to the beliefs of the Bon or shamanism and to local superstition in the northern hill areas. In any case, in Nepal Buddhism had to make accommodations with the Brahmanic tradition but was not reconquered as in India.

The Mahāyāna School of Buddhism, or the Great Vehicle, is said to have originated between the age of Aśoka and the Christian era. It appeared later than both of the well-known schools of Buddhism—the Theravāda (represented by the Pali Canon) and the Sarvāstivāda— collectively described as the Hīnayāna, or the Low Vehicle, which taught that all the individual had to do was to pursue the teaching of Buddha and seek *nirvāṇa*. Those who sought to realize this goal immediately, by aspiring to the state of *arhat*, each for himself, were the monks; and this system of discipline was known as the Śrāvakayāna, 'the Vehicle of the Disciples'. However, these schools did not rule out the possibility of realizing Buddhahood even without listening to and following the teaching of the Buddha. Those who acquired Buddhahood in this way were said to follow the Pratyeka-Buddhayāna.

One of the chief Mahāyāna *sūtras* (some of which probably date from as early as the first century A.D.) describes the *yānas* or 'careers' taught by various schools under the parable of the chariots. The Mahāyāna is like a great bullock chariot, whereas the older schools are like goat and deer chariots in this parable.

According to the relatively new doctrine of the Mahāyāna, an individual, while seeking to attain *nirvāṇa* for himself, should aim at being a Buddha so that he can preach to others and promote the welfare of all. One who sets this as a goal is a *bodhisattva* and undertakes rigorous training and discipline by which, through several rebirths, he acquires great merit and attains six virtues or perfections known as *pāramitā*. The *bodhisattva* ideal is sometimes represented by the picture of a human Buddha feeding a hungry tiger on his body. The Mahāyāna was also called the Bodhisattvayāna. The aim of this school was not to turn all disciples into saviours but to make ordinary men look up to certain great *bodhisattvas*, who, by their accumulated merit, redeem men from hell (perdition) and insure rebirth in heaven to all those who devoutly repeat the name of the favourite *bodhisattva*.

This largely accounts for the great attraction the Mahāyāna sect of Buddhism held for the simple and unsophisticated people. No wonder that it was described as a great 'bullock chariot' compared to the older sects of Buddhism. The Mahāyāna School, in order to promote the cause of Buddhism, sought to exploit in practice the instinct for prayer and devotion engendered by popular versions of Hindu worship such as the earlier versions of Shaivism and Vaishnavism. While conveniently ignoring in practice the question whether Buddha, who has attained *nirvāṇa*, can be said to exist, the Mahāyāna School of Buddhism encouraged an approach conducive to contemporary Hindu polytheism by suggesting that the Buddha who has attained *nirvāṇa* abides with other Buddhas in heavens at the ten points of space. The Mahāyāna School seems to have belatedly developed an approach to monotheism by emphasizing belief in one universal Buddha, but it is by no means the predominant doctrine. Avalokiteśvara, one of the most popular of the *bodhisattvas*, is said to take the form of Shiva or Vishnu in order to teach the doctrine to the devotee.

The metaphysical aspect of the Mahāyāna School is based on the doctrine of the Void (*śūnyata*). The Mahāyāna teachers sought to find an absolute, not merely as an ultimate goal but as a cosmic principle. The most developed system is that of Nāgārjuna, who is usually thought to have taught in the second century A.D. In his system, the doctrine of the void becomes a doctrine of relativity. Its essence is that the truth of no individual part can be maintained because nothing is real independently of the whole. This system is known as Śūnyatāvāda or Mādhyamika. The system of Asaṅga and Vasubandhu is known as Yogacāra or Vijñānavāda, in which everything is denied except consciousness (*vijñāna*). It is thus a system of subjective idealism. The systems of Mādhyamika and Vijñānavāda are important from the viewpoint of the evolution of Indian philosophy as they are elaborately refuted in the commentaries on the orthodox philosophical *sūtras*, and also because the Vedantic doctrine of *maya*, cosmic illusion, has adopted some of the principles of Vijñānavāda.

The element common to both the Mahāyāna and the Vedantic schools of philosophy is what the Indian scholastic methodology calls *samanvaya*, i.e. the institutionalized attitude of reconciling discursively contrary notions by raising them to a level of discourse where these contradictions are thought to have no validity. Those who are engaged in metaphysical speculation are content to say that when the absolute and the phenomenal are brought side by side, there is *samanvaya*, but the Tantrics insist on actually experiencing it. Both Hindu and Buddhist Tantras emphasize that the one reality which exists has to be comprehended through a process of conceptual and intuitive polarization. Both Hindu and Buddhist Tantrism, intended as short cuts to redemption, are characterized by a common outlook on fundamental absolutism and stress a psycho-experimental rather than a speculative approach. According to the tantric concept, the poles are characterized by activity and passivity and the universe operates on the basis of their interaction. The only difference between Hindu and Buddhist tantrism in this respect is that unlike in Hindu tantrism, it is the male pole that is active in Buddhist tantrism. Hindu tantrism assigned the principle of knowledge (*jñāna*) to the passive male pole and the dynamic principle of energy (*śakti*) to its female counterpart. The whole tantric movement may be described as 'psycho-experimental speculation'.

It is idle to look for differences between tantric and non-tantric forms of Buddhism and Hinduism, because Śākta and Mahāyāna

Tantrism do not contain anything which is not already there in some non-tantric schools in both religions. What Hindu and Buddhist tantrism have in common is the methodology. Tantra is merely the psycho-experimental interpretation of non-tantric lore and is certainly more value-free than the non-tantric tradition. Psycho-experimenting implies experimenting with one's own mind in the fashion of a would-be psychoanalyst rather than that of a poet or a philosopher. Like the psychoanalysts of today the tantric teachers and their pupils form a closed group for the realization of both temporal and spiritual ends.

Another feature shared by both Śākta and Mahāyāna tantrism is the interest in magic and magic formulae (*mantra*, *dhāraṇī*) and the religious use of sexual symbolism in which each Buddha or Bodhisattva is provided with a female counterpart in the same way that each god has a Śakti (female counterpart) assigned to it in the Purāṇas. The use of magic, although found in the earliest Buddhism, is not treated as a part of the doctrine. But in tantric Buddhism, the repetition of meaningless syllables is a means of acquiring merit and the continuous repetition of Avalokiteśvara's name is enough to assure rebirth in heaven.

The Vajrayāna Buddhists take for granted the identity of *nirvāṇa* and *saṃsāra* i. e., the absolute and the phenomenal modes of existence as taught and emphasized by the Māḍhyamikas. But, with regard to their ritualistic aspects or contemplative exercise (*sādhanas*), there are fundamental differences of the same kind as there are between the non-tantric monists or Śaivas, who profess the oneness of Shiva and Śakti, and the Hindu tantrics of the Śākta School. The Vajrayāna Buddhists are said to have correlated their cognitional concepts of the void (*śūnyatā*), supreme quiescent wisdom (*prajñā*), non-selfhood (*nairātma*), with the connate notions—active compassion (*karuṇā*) and means or method (*upāya*).

It is commonly believed that, unlike the Hindu Vedantic philosophers who insist on a transcendent-immanent personality principle (*ātman* or *brahman*), the Buddhists deny, at least in theory, the existence of any self or super-self. In practice, however, the Vajrayāna and for that matter, all Mahāyāna Buddhist doctrines presuppose the existence of a kind of super-self or ersatz self which cannot be defined in terms of the Hindu entity-postulating terms. According to Agehananda Bharati, the Vajrayāna and the Mahāyāna arrive at their hypostasis or quasi-entity through altogether different speculative processes and accept it, not in lieu of the Hindu entity, but in spite of it. The Buddhist dialectician derives his notion of *śūnyatā* from the premise of the denial of any entity and from that of the axiom of momentariness. On the other hand, the Hindu dialectician has a self-existing god to serve as a focus for his speculations on a self, a static entity.[1]

The Vajrayāna entity consists of *śūnyatā*, Buddhahood and such philosophical non-entities as the tantric deities, like the goddess Nairātmya (non-selfhood), personified in a multitude of ingenuously devised anthropomorphic forms. The proliferation of gods and goddesses, demons and demonesses does not seem to bother the Vajrayāna tantrics who regard them merely as the necessary anthropomorphic tools used to find out what is inside the word. Although the Buddhist concept of *śūnyatā* and the Vedantic concept of the Brahman may appear to casual observers identical intellectual constructions, they are not so because Buddhism, unlike Hinduism, does not have any ontology or metaphysics.

According to Nepali Buddhism, Buddha, the 'enlightened', a sage of the Śākya clan (*śākyamuni*), is the Buddha for the current aeon. In former aeons, other perfect and enlightened sages had taught the doctrine and in a future aeon Maitreya will be the Buddha. Ādi-Buddha (the primordial Buddha) embodies the principle of Buddhahood. This principle, when taken as operating throughout the cosmos, is represented as fivefold, with figures at the four cardinal points related to the central figure, which is resplendent and appears in the form of Buddha Vairocana (the Illuminator or the Brilliant). In a diagram or *maṇḍala* of these five Buddha Vairocana occupies the central place with reference to the other four representatives of Buddhahood.

The Buddha spirit, pervading the entire cosmos, is represented at the four cardinal points of the compass in these forms: Buddha Akṣobhya (The Imperturbable) in the east, Buddha Amitābha (The Infinite Light) in the west, Buddha Ratnasaṃbhava (The Jewel Born) in the south and Buddha Amoghasiddhi (The Unfailing Success) in the north. Each of the above five Buddhas is associated with an orientation, a cognizance, a colour, a consort (*Prajñā*), a *bodhisattva*, a spiritual heir, and even additional members of his family. Failings such as wrath, malignity, desire, envy, and stupidity are associated with each of the five Buddhas.

Idams (Sk. *iṣṭa devata*) are chosen divinities who are said to guarantee the tantric worshipper his union in Buddhahood with any one of the five Buddhas with whom his human failing is associated. Heruka implies the fierce aspect of a Buddha. Each of the five Buddhas has his Heruka aspect, and each Heruka has several forms. Through the tantric mechanism of these Heruka-Idams the human failing is changed into the special kind of wisdom represented by the particular Buddha. This explains the fierce forms of Akṣobhya and the different forms of Heruka such as Hevajra and Saṃvara.

Chart 1

The Five Buddhas (Pañcabuddha, Pañcatathāgata)

Buddha	Viarocana (Brilliant)	Akṣobhya (Impertur-able)	Ratnasaṃbhava (Jewel-born)	Amitābha (Infinite Light)	Amoghasiddhi (Unfailing Success)
Consort	Vajradhā-tiśvarī	Locanā	Māmakī	Paṇḍāra-vasinī	Tārā
Position	Centre	East	South	West	North
Colour	White	Blue	Yellow	Red	Green
Mudra (Cogni-zance)	Dharma-cakra (Teaching)	Bhūmi-sparsa (Calling to Witness)	Varada (Giving)	Dhyāna (Meditation)	Abhaya (Fearless-ness)
Symbol	Cakra (Wheel)	Vajra	Ratna (Jewel)	Padma (Lotus)	Khaḍga (Sword)
Vehicle	Lion	Elephant	Horse	Peacock	Garuda
Earthly Buddha	Krakuc-chanda	Kanaka-muni	Kāśyapa	Gautama Sākyamuni	Maitreya
Bodhi-sattva (Spiritual Heir)	Samanta-bhadra	Vajrapāni	Ratnapāni	Avalokit-eśvara	Viśvapāni
Element	Space	Earth	Water	Fire	Air
Human Personality	Concious-ness	Form	Feeling	Perception	Impulses
Five Aspects of Wisdom	Pure-Absolute	Mirror-like	Discrimi-natory	Homo-genous	Active
Evil	Ignorance	Wrath	Desire	Passions	Envy

This explains the fierce forms of Akṣobhya and the different forms Heruka such as Hevajra and Saṃvara.

An acquaintance with the general concept of the Five Buddhas (*pañca-buddha* or *pañca-tathāgata*) is essential, not only to the understanding and appreciation of the later forms of Buddhism found in Nepal but also to the symbolism of Nepali art and sculpture. Chart 1 presents a summary view of the scheme of the Buddhas.

Śākyamuni himself is said to have accepted three of the above mentioned mortal Buddhas or Tathagatas as his predecessors: Krakuchanda, Kāśyapa and Kanakamuni. Vipaśya, Sikhi, and Viśvabhu are also mentioned in order of succession as the forerunners of Śakyamuni's predecessors. Thus, there are seven well-known Tathāgata or Buddhas, including Gautama Buddha, but the list can be interminably drawn further back. Although these Tathāgatas or Buddhas (with the exception of Maitreya), are without historical foundation, all of them are sometimes described as the 'historical' Buddhas merely to indicate the chronological order of their appearance on earth. As 'historical' they are in contradistinction to the Five Transcendent Buddhas who do not appear on this earth.

From the eleventh to the fourteenth century, Nepal became a testing ground for different systems of religious thought and practice imported from India. The influence of the Brahminical reformist movement, led by Śaṅkarācārya of South India, penetrated into Nepal at about the same time as the esoteric practice of Tantrism based on the earlier Śaiva and Śākta cults and on Buddhist Mahāyāna formalism. Nepal became not only a focal point where these divergent religious practices converged, but also a melting pot of different kinds of religious thought and rituals which were transmogrified into the Nepali version of Vajrayāna.

Despite the fact that Hindu and Buddhist tantras and their respective synthetic products remained separate from one another, the Vajrayāna, especially in its local manifestation, showed a remarkable capacity for assimilating most of the significant traits of religious evolution in Nepal. The notion of the thunderbolt as a phallus penetrating the void which is represented by the female generative organ, and the elements of superstition and magic common to all primitive religions largely accounted for the popularity of the Vajrayāna among the masses. However, it is not certain to this day whether non-Buddhist Indian, tantric or similar ideas were responsible for the creation of the Vajrayāna school, which was first introduced in Nepal and then transplanted to Tibet, or whether the left-handed (*vāma mārgī*) tantric schools owed to Buddhism the tantric notions using sexual polarity.

After duly pointing out that Buddhism was a mass religion and that it was not easy for the masses to comprehend the real philosophical significance of Prajñā, Upāya and Nirvaṇa, Benoytosh Bhattacharya presents the problem in simple terms:

> The Bodhi Chitta merges in Niratma and there remains in eternal bliss (Mahasukha). The word 'Niratma,' it may be noted, is in the feminine, the Niratma is therefore a Devi, in whose embrace the Bodhi Chitta remains. The masses will understand the

significance of Nairatma, and this feminine aspect—an outcome of Mahasukha Doctrine—in the doctrine of Nirvana gave rise to Vajrayāna.[2]

Certain features of Vajrayāna Tantra might have some analogues in pre-Buddhist Tibet and also in the era of the pre-Aryan Paśupata cult in the Kathmandu Valley. The Vajrayāna cult, which came originally from Bengal and Bihar, in its Nepali version, served as a means of bringing together some of the features of both the Hindu Śākta and Buddhist Mahāyāna traditions as modified by local conditions. For example, notwithstanding the fact that Buddhist tantric tradition assigns a passive function to female goddesses, in the Nepali and Tibetan versions of the Vajrayāna, goddesses like Aparājita (The Invincible) and Vajravarāhī (The Adamantine Sow) play a relatively more active role compared to traditional Mahāyāna tantric goddesses. Their role is similar to that of the Śaktis, or the dynamic female energies, in the Hindu or Śākta Tantric tradition. However, in keeping with the accepted tradition of Mahāyāna Tantrism, the Nepali and Tibetan versions of the Vajrayāna have also adopted the passive goddesses like Tārā or Locanā and have retained the traditional Mahāyāna goddesses like Prajñāpāramitā ('Perfection of Wisdom') and Nairitya ('Non-self-hood').

There had always been an exchange of students and teachers between Nepal and the Buddhist universities of Bihar and Bengal. After the fall of the Pala and the Sena dynasty in Bengal, and of the Karnataka dynasty of Tirhut to the successive waves of Muslim invasion between the ninth and the fourteenth centuries, tantric teachers from Bengal and Mithila sought sanctuary in Nepal. Great teachers of Buddhism, such as Śāntarakṣita and Padmasaṃbhava in the eighth century, and Atiśa in the eleventh century, came to Nepal and then went on to Tibet where they made lasting contributions to Tibetan Buddhism.

Buddhism continued to penetrate into the Kathmandu Valley through its intellectuals. Thus Nepal served as a relay-station for transmitting Buddhism across the Himalaya, and, for a long time, Nepal supplied teachers and artists to Tibet. Tibetan abbots and princes sent for Nepali artists, sculptors and craftsmen to beautify their temples with frescoes, to cast statues or to copy early Buddhist manuscripts. Tibetan monks learned Sanskrit from Nepali teachers of Buddhism and translated into their own language the masterpieces of Buddhist ritualistic literature. Nepal therefore served as a channel for southern influences to penetrate to the north. As Professor Tucci, an authority on Indo-Tibetan cultural relations says, 'Nepal brought the task of mediation between Indian and Tibetan cultures to perfection'.[3]

In the evolution of the religious synthesis represented by the cult of the Vajrayāna there were initially clashes between upholders of the orthodox Brahminical tradition and those of Mahāyāna ritualism. The puritanic zeal with which Śaṅkarācārya's movement for Brahmanic revival was conducted led to resistance from the followers of Mahāyāna Buddhism. There is a popular legend about the massacre of seven hundred and seventy Brahmans by Buddhists. Although doubtless an exaggeration, the story offers a clue to the reactions of the indigenous followers of Buddhism to the provocation caused by the aggressive disciples of Śaṅkarācārya.

However, such religious antagonism did not last long. Brahmanic tradition, and the deities of ritualistic Buddhism that figured in the original Vajrayāna cult were gradually adopted and worshipped, even by the descendants of the upholders of the orthodox Brahminical faith. The disappearance of Buddhist monasteries and monastic life in Nepal, which is generally ascribed to the subsequent predominance of Hinduism, also resulted from the growth of the Vajrayāna tradition which did not give to celibacy the same importance as the earlier Buddhists.

Nine books of Mahāyāna Buddhism became the canon of the Buddhists of the Kathmandu Valley. They were: *Aṣṭasāhasrikā Prajñāpāramitā* ('The Perfection of Wisdom in Eight Thousand Stanzas'), *Gandhavyūha* ('Blossom Decoration'), *Daśabhūmisūtra* ('The Ten-Character Field'), *Samādhirājasūtra* ('The Principal Book of Concentration'), *Laṅkāvatāra Sūtra*' ('Scripture Concerning Buddha's Entry into Lanka'), *Saddharmapuṇḍarika* ('The Lotus of the Good Law'), *Lalitavistara* ('Buddha's Boyhood'), *Suvarnaprabāsasūtra* ('Golden Illumination'), *Tathāgata Gūhyaka* ('Secret Doctrine of the Tathāgata'). Abstract notions of Mahāyāna Buddhism assumed concrete forms like Hindu gods and goddesses. Some of the most popular in Nepal were: Prajñāpāramitā (Perfection of Wisdom), Nāmasaṇgīti (Harmony of Name), Pañcarakṣa-Maṇḍala (Pattern For Five-Fold Protection), and Nairātma (Non-Self-Hood), a fierce goddess representing The Void (śūnyatā).

Atiśa (Dipaṅkara Śrījñāna), a famous Buddhist teacher from India, gave formal shape to Vajrayāna in the eleventh century, and by the fourteenth century it had become fully developed. Simple religious and social life, based on a trinity of Buddha, Dharma (Religion), and Saṅgha (Organization), was replaced in the casteless Buddhist society by an ecclesiastical hierarchy resembling the Hindu caste structure. In Tibet,

Buddhism, under the influence of tantrism, developed into Lamaism with its belief in reincarnate Lamas and other ritualistic formalities, while in Nepal Vajrayāna became more and more associated with the Brahminical traditions.

Tantrism is based on texts called Tantra, works of revelation. It prescribes rites by which Knowledge of the Self (*ātmajñāna*) or Buddhahood (Enlightenment) can be attained. Tantrism influenced Hinduism and Buddhism through the introduction of an esoteric system of rites. Hinduism, as influenced by Tantrism, took the form of ritualistic worship of Śakti as a symbol of dynamic female energy. Thus, the pre-Aryan elements of Hinduism, such as the worship of the Linga or the Phallus and the adoration of the female generative organ as a symbol of the cosmic mother, were absorbed by Tantrism.

The cult of the Linga was so prevalent in the religious symbiosis achieved in Nepal that even Buddhism could not escape its influence. The Yoni, or the female sex-organ, became the symbol of the cosmic waters, representing the turbulent movement of the infinite possibilities of being, whereas the Linga represented emergence from this turbulence of the lotus which symbolized the ordered life with its culmination in spiritual serenity. Vajrayāna, which was derived from the *mahāsukha* doctrine and sought to sublimate sensuous or even sensual enjoyment, merely presented the same principle in another form, when it regarded the Vajra or thunderbolt as the means of penetrating the void or *śūnyatā* in the process of securing release from the bond of worldly enjoyment in order to attain *nirvāṇa* (desirelessness).

The ultimate objective of those initiated into the practice of tantric rites was to merge the individual self into the universal or divine self, that is, to become one with god. It symbolized the union of the male and the female cosmic principles, Puruṣa and Śakti, manifesting themselves in the creation of the world (*līla*). The union also evoked a sense of divine unity by underlining the sexual dualism of the deity as exemplified by the concept of a half-man and half-woman image (*ardhanārīśvara*). The images of many tantric divinities, such as those known to the Tibetans and the Chinese as Yab-Yum (Father-Mother) and Yang-Yin (Active Male and Female Principles) respectively, are similar to what the Śaiva schools define as Śiva-Śakti. All of them symbolize, in different forms, the union of man with the supreme principle of being.

This conception of oneness is not confined to Nepali and Tibetan Buddhism, but is familiar also to the philosophical tradition enshrined in the Brāhmaṇas and Upaṇiṣadas. In the Purāṇas also, each god has a

Śakti assigned to him. Principal among the Śaktis is Pārvati, the consort of Shiva. She is widely worshipped in the form of Kālī or Dūrgā as a Mother Goddess. Pictures of Umā-Maheśvara show the god Shiva in the company of his Śakti, Umā (Pārvati).

Buddhism, in spite of its essentially moralistic doctrine, developed into the ritualistic cult of the union of *upāya* (means or method) with the female principle, *prajñā* (gnosis or quiescent wisdom) under tantric influence. The conception of Idam Saṃvara or Hevajra, commonly reproduced in Nepali bronzes and paintings, visualizes the Heruka or fierce aspect of Buddha in union with his female partner, Vajravarāhī, the cosmic mother, in the form of the Adamantine Sow. It is with a mixed feeling of love and fear that the illiterate masses of the people worship the cosmic mother, who is represented in various mild and terrible forms in the temples of Nepal. This cosmic mother in various manifestations characterized by postures or symbols, joyous or horrendous, provides profound insights to keen observers and devotees of 'becoming' , which works through the dialectic of birth and death, procreation and elimination, these two phases being inextricably bound up with each other, even in the realm of *māyā* or the perpetual state of flux, through the magical operation of the Śakti, producing the supreme synthesis of *eros* or *kāma* and *thanatos*, the shadow of death.

Tantrism, at its best, preached that like *yoga* or spiritual discipline, the path of *bhoga*, or sexual enjoyment, could also lead to the union of 'substance' with 'essence' or the identification of the *ātma* with Brahma. The sexual symbolism employed for the interpretation of tantric philosophy or for the explanation of the various stages of divine epiphany contemplated therein were not intelligible to the non-initiates. The *pañcamakāras* or 'five words beginning with the letter "m"' (*madya* wine, *matsya* fish, *māṃsa* meat, *mudrā* parched kidney bean, *maithuna* copulation) have two meanings: the literal and the esoteric. For example, *māṃsa* could mean flesh or religious formula, *matsya* fish or senses, *madya,* wine or nectar, *mudrā* an aphrodisiac or the refulgent lotus which in the practice of *yoga,* glows like a dazzling flame on top of the head, and finally *maithuna* coitus or the consummation of *yoga*, i.e. the attainment of supreme wisdom. As the number of initiates decreased, the tantric insistence on the *makāras* was misunderstood, notwithstanding the repeated warnings of the masters of tantra that the books of tantra were secret and meant only for those who were properly initiated by qualified masters.

It was not only the lack of proper interpretation that could be held responsible for the decline of tantrism. A woman, or especially a virgin, was at first exalted to the position of a living goddess by making her an object of solemn meditation. But in due course, this resulted in the recommendation for copulation in the maṇḍapa or psychocosmogram with a view to giving the initiate an actual experience of transcending the level of worldly pain and pleasure and experiencing a state of happiness or ecstasy even though for a few moments. The idea, however, was to enable the initiate to attain, by gradual stages, a permanent state of bliss, the first experience of which he had already acquired from sexual union with the object of his meditation. This might have sublimated the sexual practice and symbolism by placing it on the same level as the process of 'transference' or 'transfiguration' in religious or yogic contemplation. Unfortunately, it also led to the wide prevalence of deviant forms of sexual practice.

Not all tantras or all sections of the tantric texts served merely as a guide to salvation. They contained chapters on magic and discussed ways of dominating the world, by the restoration of peace and the destruction of enemies, the warding off of dangers, the performance of terrible deeds, the submission of another person's will (especially a woman's) to one's own. Certain tantras contained chapters on medicine along with those which gave prescriptions for aphrodisiacs and pills intended for delaying ejaculation. Tantric rites, in the hands of unscrupulous practitioners degenerated into a form of sorcery and were practised to appease evil spirits. This led to the subsequent decline of tantrism. However, the Vajrayāna cult, which combined the mystic and devotional features of Shaivism and Vaishnavism with the primitive elements of magic, superstition, and sensuous enjoyment, easily captivated the minds of the common people for a long time.

It cannot be stated definitely when tantrism was developed or when it entered Nepal, but it had appeared there in an embryonic stage as early as the seventh and eighth centuries. During the fourteenth and fifteenth centuries untouchables like Pores were admitted, as votaries and caretakers, into the temples of the goddesses on the banks of the cremation rivers and lonely places, thus allowing them the right of participation in the worship of the cosmic mother for their salvation. Kathmandu's eight Kalikas, Bhadgaun's eight Matrikas and Patan's eight Kumaris date back to the sixteenth century, and by this time many new gods and goddesses had come into existence under the impact of tantrism.

A large variety of gods and goddesses, saints and *siddhas* from both Buddhist and Hindu pantheons were introduced into Nepal and were absorbed into the Vajrayāna cult as it gradually attained its full development. In addition to the Five Buddhas of the Mahāyāna pantheon,

Dhṛtarāṣṭra, Vīrudhaka, Vīrupakṣa, and Vaiśravaṇa became the guardians of the four quarters (*catur mahārāja*), and the ten guardians of the directions (daśalokapāla) were Indra, Yama, Varuṇa, Kubera, Iśāna, Agni, Nairtya, Vāyu, Brahma and Krishna. The eighty-four Vajrayāna *siddhas* known in Tibet were also known in Nepal but eight of them became quite popular: Luipā, Nāgārjuna, Virūpā, Kukuripā, Karṇaripā, Ghantapā, Nāropā, and Sabaripā. They were pictured with meditative postures slightly different from those of the Tibetan *siddhas* of the same time.

The worship of goddesses of all kinds came into vogue in medieval Nepal under the influence of tantrism. Pārvatī, consort of Shiva, began to be worshipped in many manifestations. The so called *aṣṭamātṛka* group of eight goddesses associated with certain failings were Brahmayāṇi (Arrogance), Kumarī (Chimera), Rudrayāṇī (Fear), Vaiṣṇavī (Greed), Varāhī (Envy), Indrayāṇi (Fault-finding with Evil Design), Chamuṇḍā (Eavesdropping) and Mahālakṣmī (Wealth and Prosperity) with other variation of eight names such as Dūrgā, Brahmānī, Kumarī, Vaiṣṇavī, Maheśvarī, Varāhī and Narasiṃhī. Pārvatī became Tārā in the Buddhist cult of Vajrayāna. The goddesses common to both Śākta and Buddhist tantras are Vajravarāhī, Vajrayoginī or Ugratārā, Vijayeśvarī, Vidyadharī, Dakṣiṇakālī, Chinnamaṣṭikā, Chandeśvarī, Gūhyeśvarī, Sobhābhagavati, Annapurṇa, Mahālakṣmī, and Mahāsarasvati.

Among the female deities of local origin may be mentioned Lumāḍī (Bhadrakālī), Mahipī (Maheśvarī), Maitidevī, Kaṅga Ajimā (Kaṅkeśvarī), Lutumārī (Indrayāṇī), Manthalidevī (Martyeśvarī). All of them are connected with the ancient cult of the mother-goddess or the cosmic mother, notwithstanding later attempts to identify them with the Śākta goddesses. Of the local deities, special mention must be made of Hāriti Ajimā and Mapatadevā (Ākāśadevī) as both of them were said to have been fond of killing children for their food until their own children were carried away by Buddha or Visnu to teach them the lesson that other children are as dear to their parents as their own children are to these two goddesses. They eventually received their children back with the understanding that they would leave other people's children unharmed. This Hāriti-Ajimā, or Śitalā, is the popular goddess of smallpox who is shown as a deity who 'rides on a donkey, has such emblems as a sweeping broom and a pitcher, and is adorned with a winnowing fan on her head.' Naradevī, Raktakālī, Maṇi Maiju, Chandeśvarī (of Tokha and Banepa), Rudrayāṇī of Khokana and Harisiddhi (Ajimādevāta) were important centers for tantric rites where at one time, it is said, human sacrifices were made.

The cult of Taleju or, Mānesvarī, the tutelary goddess of the later Mallas, reached its full development in the fourteenth century. During the fourteenth and the fifteenth centuries Jhaṅkeśvarī, Rājarājeśvarī, and Kubjikā were worshipped by the feudal chiefs of Pharping as their tutelary goddesses. The legend 'Lokanātha' is embossed on the coins of the Patan kings. Lokanātha (Padmapāṇi Lokeśvara) is identified with Matsyendranatha, and Taleju with Śaiva Dūrgā and the Buddhist Tārā. The temple of Budhanilakantha is dedicated to Vishnu as are the four famous Narayana temples of Changu, Ichangu, Sikhara, and Visankhu.

The people of medieval Nepal lived in mortal fear of a myriad of demons and deities, ogres and ogresses, supernatural beings and godly creatures, ghosts and evil spirits against whom they needed constant protection from superior gods and goddesses, who, in their turn, were supposed to be appeased and propitiated much in the same way as ordinary human beings. To those who lived in medieval times the external world was entirely peopled with ghostly beings, airy nothings, shapeless and bodiless apparitions that were largely the creation of their imaginations. Among these creatures of fantasy, the malignant and evil ones easily outnumbered the benevolent and the good. As a means of appeasing the malignant spirits and gaining the blessings of the benevolent ones, magic, incantation and esoteric rites had a great attraction for the simple-minded people living in an atmosphere surcharged with a feeling of blind faith and superstition.

The introduction of numerous rites and the proliferation of gods and goddesses diluted the philosophical and mystical elements of both Buddhism and Brahmanism. Both these religions began to be treated merely as guides to the performance of religious rites to propitiate gods and goddesses with the object of attaining happiness both in this life and the next. This led the people to conceive of gods as human beings with human weaknesses such as malice, wrath, envy and greed. The tantras claimed to provide the mechanism for the transformation of those apparent human failings on the part of gods into real blessings for the initiates. Had it not been for the Vajrayāna impact on Buddhism, the latter would have been swept away by the rising tide of Brahmanism in Nepal and Bengal as in the rest of the Indo-Gangetic plains. The influence of Vajrayāna practices can be felt not only on the evolution of religious culture but also on art, architecture, and learning during the period. The later Śaiva or Hindu predominance merely consolidated the process which Vajrayāna had set in motion.

According to Percival Landon, three factors played an important role in the making of the Nepali pantheon. He states,

> The Nepalese pantheon contains three elements: firstly, aboriginal deities such as the Nagas and the other nature spirits; definitely Buddhist deities or Bodhisattvas of whom Manjusri receives the most honour; and thirdly, Hindu deities such as Ganesh or Krishna. The popular deity Machhendranata or Matsyendranata, appears to combine all these elements in his own person.[4]

Matsyendranātha who is identified with Avalokiteśvara or Padmapāṇi Lokeśvara, the spiritual heir of the Buddha Amitābha has become a legendary figure in Nepali religious life. The legend has it that he redeemed the parched valley after a long period of drought by making Gorakhanātha rise from his seat of Nāgas (serpents) to give the valley the much sought-after rain. According to the Buddhist accounts, the gods of the Hindu pantheon showered praise on Avalokiteśvara for performing this remarkable feat, whereas the Hindu version, while admitting that Matsyendranātha was the tutor of Gorakhanātha makes the latter the central figure of the legend. The cart festival of Matsyendranātha is attended by both Hindus and Buddhists with equal reverence and enthusiasm.

Although, as we have seen the fierce manifestations of Buddha are depicted trampling on the Hindu gods, Brahma, Indra, Visnu, and Shiva as Evil ones (*māras*) no hostile feeling is in evidence between the tantric Buddhists and the Hindus, probably because the latter have accepted Buddha himself as one of the ten incarnations of the Hindu god. Percival Landon has rightly pointed out that 'of odium theologicum there is little in Nepal because any differences between these two interwoven faiths would more probably be caused by a political than a religious issue.'[5]

NOTES

1. Agehananda Bharati, *The Tantric Tradition*, London, Rider, 1965, p. 26.
2. Benoytosh Bhattacharyya, *An Introduction to Buddhist Esotersim*, Varanasi, Chowkhamba, 1964, p. 27.
3. G. Tucci, *Nepal—The Discovery of the Malla*, London, E.P. Dutton, 1962, p. 83.
4. Percival Landon, *Nepal*, London, Constable, 1928, II, p. 216.
5. *Ibid.*, p. 218.

CHAPTER XIII

MEDIEVAL ART AND ARCHITECTURE

Religion has always provided Nepali art and architecture with inspiration and motifs. However, this is not to minimize the quality of Nepali artistic sensibility. Percy Brown has made the following observation on the artistic achievement of the Nepalis:

> The temples and public buildings reveal such a wealth of fine and applied art that it is clear that the inhabitants of the valley from a very early period possessed a keen appreciation of the aesthetic. This admirable trait in the Newar national character appears to have been instinctive, while at the same time both their rulers (the Mallas and the Shahs) seem to have fostered and encouraged this feeling for art to its fullest extent. The result of this favourable combination of circumstances is that Nepal may claim to have critically developed a distinctive art of its own, in other words, a Nepalese school of art.[1]

Recent expeditions into remote Nepal, close to the Tibetan border, have led to the discovery of architectural relics and monuments. Their styles do not seem to differ in the main from those in the Kathmandu Valley, which has been the epicentre of Nepali art and architecture. The creative genius of Newari artists and artisans in various fields has earned for Nepali schools a place of respect and renown in the history of Asian art. During the past half century archaeological surveys and excavations have uncovered the pre-Ashokan ruins of Kapilavastu in the mid-western tarai, near Rupandehi and Tilaurakot. Similarly, ruins of the old Kingdom of Simraungarh have been discovered in the central tarai. It is clear that Nepali architectural styles have influenced several other Asian countries including China, India and Burma.

Nepal offers two main styles in architecture: the *caitya* style and the so-called pagoda, or multi-roofed style. The oldest structures in the Kathmandu Valley are specimens of the *caitya* style. Examples of these are the *stūpas* found in the town of Lalitpur, two or three miles to the south of Kathmandu. There were five *stūpas*, four at the cardinal points outside the city and one, no longer extant, at its centre. These are plain, dome-like structures of earth and brick on a plinth built of the same materials and are devoid of any decoration or ornamentation except for a chapel on the top.

The chapel is said to have been dedicated to Vairocana, one of the five Buddhas, and the chapels at the four cardinal points of the compass are dedicated to the four other forms of Buddha: Akṣobhya, Amitābha, Ratnasaṃbhava and Amoghasiddhi. The one at the centre stands on a base made of stone and has a summit consisting of a cube-shaped canopy formed of semi-circular rings or arches which hold and sustain a parasol on a tripod of metal.

Two of the best known *stūpas* in the Kathmandu Valley are those of Swayambhu and Bauddhanath, which are situated at the western and north-eastern outskirts of Kathmandu respectively. According to the *Gopālarājavaṃśāvalī* Swayambhu was founded by King Vṛsadeva, the great-grandfather of King Mānadeva, about the beginning of the fifth century. A damaged stone inscription discovered in the grounds at Swayambhu seems to confirm this. Because of its antiquity all kinds of religious myths and legends have grown up around it. Like Devapatan in the vicinity of the famous Pashupatinath temple, the Swayambhu area has been an important centre of cultural activities for a period of about sixteen hundred years.

While the Swayambhu *stūpa* may have had its origin as a standard Mahāyāna Buddhist shrine, it gradually acquired many features of tantric Buddhism and has grown into a place of worship for Nepali Hindus as well. Located on a hillock, Swayambhu has within its holy precincts quite a number of *caityas*, multi-roofed temples and other shrines. According to legend the hillock was once marked by an eternally burning and self existent flame (*svayaṃbhu*). In a later age the *stūpa* was built over the eternal flame as a permanent monument. To the north-west of the *stūpa* is the shrine of Hāriti-Ajimā, the protectress against smallpox. Though Hāriti is of Buddhist origin, the image is worshipped by Hindus alike who refer to her either by the generic name of Ajimā ('Grandmother') or the Hindu name Śitalā. A large number of lingams or phallic emblems scattered around the area are either covered as *caityas* or have the faces of the four Buddhas carved on them. The copper thunderbolt (*vajra*), placed at the top of the stairs to the east overlooking the valley, and the two white *śikhara* temples on either side of it are tantric in inspiration and were erected by King Pratāpa Malla of Kathmandu. On a secondary hillock to the west of the Swayambhu *stūpa* stands a shrine to Mañjuśrī. The shrine consists of a *stūpa* with the western side enlarged to house an image of Padmapāṇi Lokeśvara. In front of this image are a pair of feet which represent Mañjuśrī. The shrine is frequented by large numbers of both Buddhists and Hindus, who worship not Mañjuśrī but Sarasvati. These two are constantly conflated in the Valley and this is one of the few instances where Hinduism and Buddhism get thoroughly mixed. This is understandable, as Mañjuśrī and Sarasvati are both deities of learning or wisdom. Later tantric texts tried to reconcile the two by saying that Sarasvati is the wife of Mañjuśrī.

The Bauddhanath *stūpa*, sometimes called the Khāsa *Caitya*, is more distinctively Tibetan in character and surrounding. It is mentioned in the *Gopālarājavaṃśāvalī* which attributes its foundation to King Śivadeva (c. A.D. 590-604), though another chronicle attributes it to King Mānadeva (A.D. 464-505). However, available historical records at the site go back only to medieval times. The present distinctively Tibetan character of the shrine dates to this period when it became a shrine of people of Tibetan culture who then renovated and expanded the shrine. Perhaps by that time it had been abandoned by the Newar Buddhists who now have no ritual connections with the shrine.

Both the Swayambhu and the Bauddhanath *stūpas* are surrounded on all sides by houses which are inhabited, not by the monks as in former times, but mostly by the laity. Despite their claims to a much earlier origin, those *stūpas* do not appear to be as old as the *stūpas* at Lalitpur, most probably a result of successive renovations which were more in keeping with the Tibetan than the Nepali tradition in architecture.

Miniature *stūpas* are often called *caityas* in Nepal, though the two Sanskrit terms have the same meaning. These *caityas* are of the same design and execution as the larger monuments. The site of a *caitya* is often called 'Ci-bāhā' today, a term derived from a shortening of the Sanskrit term *caitya-bhaṭṭāraka* ('revered *caitya*'). The Dhanadeu Caitya at Chabel (a large monument despite its name) and the numerous small *caityas* and images of the Buddha and Bodhisattvas surrounding it are remarkable for their antiquity and also for their artistic design which is of the highest order. The Dhanadeu Caitya is said to have been founded by King Dharmadeva, the father of Mānadeva. The still current name of Dhanadeu is a corruption of his name, and the name is attested to by a number of still extant inscriptions at the site which refer to the monastery which existed there as the Dharmadeva-Caitya Vihāra. The exquisite image of the Buddha to the side of the *caitya* is estimated to be of the fifth century and the small *caityas* have been accurately dated to the seventh century.

While *stūpas* are also found in India and the *stūpas* at Patan bear a striking resemblance to the one at Sanchi in India, the multi-roofed, or so-called pagoda style, temple architecture has come to be recognized as quintessentially Nepali. Recent study and research, however, has shown both the antiquity of this style and its dependence on Indian art. The multi-roofed style of temple, typified by the Pashupati temple, shows a number of unique features which were established some time before A.D. 400 and have been carried on faithfully since that time. These features all derive from north India and the typical brick structure of the Nepalese temple with its forward sloping roofs derives entirely from the art of the Kusana period in India. Some features from the later Gupta period were subsequently incorporated, but the basic structure has remained the same. Later developments in India added a few incidental features, but after the Muslim invasions of the 13th century inspiration from north India ceased and the style was handed on to the builders of the Malla period unchanged as it has remained to the present day.[2]

Some authorities have argued that the Nepali multi-roofed style of temple antedates the development of the pagoda style of architecture in China. Sylvain Levi was of the opinion that the earliest specimens of the pagoda style now extant in Nepal are much earlier than the oldest known pagodas in China. This can hardly be held any longer, as the oldest extant temples of the Valley date to the 13th century. The fact that Wang Hsuan Tse, a seventh-century emissary to Nepal, expressed his astonishment at the sight of the pagoda-like structures in Nepal seems to have led Levi to conclude that this style was unknown in China at the time.

King Bhūpatīndra Malla (c. 1696-1722) of Bhadgaun will forever be remembered for the 'five-roofed' or Nyātapola, temple which he built in Bhadgaun and dedicated to the goddess Bhavani. This temple is a typical example of Nepali temple architecture. This type of structure has roofs in tiers and may have as many as six storeys. The base is a terraced platform of stones which has as many stages or folds as there are storeys. The Nyātapola temple has a five-fold base of rectangular terraces with a steep stone-paved stairway watched over by five conventional pairs of men, elephants, lions and two other kinds of deities. At the top, a square chamber enclosed by a colonnade of wooden poles and pillars sustains the lowest and the heaviest roof. The floor of each of these storeys (surmounting one another) is a square entablature of brick which goes on diminishing in size and area until the structure reaches the fifth or the uppermost roof with a gold finial atop. The topmost roof is of gilded copper. Each of the roofs is sustained by struts projecting at an angle of about forty-five degrees from the entablature which rests for support on the pillars of the lower storey. Both the graceful carvings in relief or in the round and the vigorous sculptures that decorate the struts are characteristic of Nepali architecture in general. As a matter of fact, the Nyātapola temple is not as beautifully carved as the Changunarayana temple or even some of the other temples. The temple of Changunarayana, to the north of Thimi, and the Matsyendranātha temple in Lalitpur may also be cited as typical examples of this style of temple architecture.

The well known Hindu temple of Pashupati is perhaps the most typical of the Nepalese temples. Although the image and temple of Pashupatinath, the guardian deity of Nepal, are known for their great antiquity and are said to have existed before 533 A.D., they have not always existed in their present form. They were damaged and destroyed by Shamshu-din Iliyas, who invaded the Kathmandu Valley in 1349A.D. According to the available stone-inscriptions, the temple of Pasupatinath was reconstructed in 1381 by Jayasiṃharāma Varddhana, the leading feudatory of Banepa, during the time of Jayasthiti Malla. Further renovations took place in the late Malla period, and the temple was last extensively renovated in 1967.

There is no dearth of references in religious literature to Gūhyeśvarī, the most esteemed and the holiest of the goddesses of the śākta tradition, and this can be cited as proof of her antiquity and holiness. However, the first historical record available at the site of the temple of Gūhyeśvarī is the stone-inscription of King Pratāpa Malla of Kathmandu, dated A.D.1660. This inscription mentions a few donations made by him. A statue of King Pratāpa Malla stands to this day by the side of the temple.

The temples of Taleju, the tutelary goddess of the Malla rulers of the medieval period, from the fourteenth to the eighteenth centuries, are also done in the typical Nepali style. An image and temple of Taleju was first established at Bhadgaun in the early fourteenth century. King Ratna Malla and King Siddhinarasiṃha Malla are also said to have set up temples of Taleju in the vicinity of the royal palaces at Kathmandu and Patan respectively. King Mahendra Malla of Kathmandu is credited with building the present temple of Taleju at Kathmandu. The three

Taleju temples differ in plan and size, but the Kathmandu temple is the most impressive of all. The Patan temple is characterised by simplicity and elegance whereas the one at Bhadgaun is an unadorned structure built like an ordinary house. The Bhadgaun temple has two separate sanctums of the goddess in the Taleju quadrangle inside the Bhadgaun Royal Palace.

Nepali architectural ornamentation is rich and varied. Cornices crowning windows and doors, lintels and sills, beams, struts and brackets supporting roof projections and eaves overhanging the walls of the structure are decorated with either floral arabesques or with images of deities. The windows, which are more or less of a square shape, are screened with a finely wrought frame of trellis and appear to be slightly slanted. An architrave, covered with images of deities in bold relief, adorns the doorway which has a gilded copper finial (*kalaśa*) at the centre. The golden door of the Bhadgaun palace and the doorway of the Changunarayana temple are the finest specimens of this kind of work. The entire inside of this temple is also exquisitely decorated with fine specimens of wood carving. Besides the temples, quite a number of old palaces and houses in the Kathmandu Valley are done in the typical style of architecture.

The traditional houses, usually built of plain red brick, are not as high as the temples. But even the houses have seldom less than three storeys and usually display a profusion of wooden struts, pillars, eaves, arches and spandrels providing a wide scope for the use of Newari talents in wood-carving. However, during the past century there has been a growing tendency to ignore traditional Nepali architectural styles in the construction of both religious and residential buildings. The Rana palaces show no evidence of the traditional Nepali style of architecture, but are entirely subject to western influences; and much new housing built in the last four decades also ignores indigenous styles.

The squares in front of the old royal palaces in every one of the three cities in the Kathmandu Valley were planned and laid out with great artistic skill. These squares have excited the admiration of many a foreign visitor. Impressed by the beauty and antiquity of the Darbar (palace) Square in Bhadgaun E. Alexander Powell, a globe-trotting western visitor, pays glowing tribute to it in the following words:

> The golden temples of Siam, the pagodas of the summer palace in Peking, the sculpture-crowded terraces of Boroboedor, the grotesque structures which line the bank of the Ganges at Benares, Samarkand's wealth of colours, the carvings at Angkor, the torii of

> the Shinto sanctuaries in Japan—Bhatgaon holds vague suggestions of them all without actually resembling any of them. I who have seen all, or nearly all, the famous cities and buildings of the world, give you my word that were there nothing else in Nepal save the Durbar Square of Bhatgaon it would still be amply worth making a journey half-way round the globe to see. . . .
>
> From the standpoint of the architect and the artist, Bhatgaon is a cave of Aladdin. It is a jumble of architectural fantasies, a vast storehouse of the treasures of Newar art. In the Durbar Square alone are enough carvings and statues to fill a score of great museums to overflowing. For here, in this forgotten valley, artist-priests and master-craftsmen have been at work unceasingly for generations beyond reckoning. Here the architectures of two great religions meet and mingle. Here have been concentrated the artistic energies of a nation. Here is to be found a living fragment of India as it must have been in those glowing, glorious, far-off days before the Moslem came.[3]

The squares in front of the old royal palaces at Lalitpur and Kathmandu are also equally impressive and beautiful. Apart from the architectural magnificence of the palaces themselves, the squares present a colourful array of temples, shrines, images, and idols, sculptured pillars and statuaries, royal baths and fountains all of which enhance the special charm and beauty of the general spectacle.

Sculpture

Nepali sculpture in the early medieval period was influenced by both South Indian and Eastern Indian traditions. The Sena rulers originally belonged to the Deccan. Nānyadeva came from Karnataka, in the same region, and conquered a portion of North Bihar at the edge of the Nepal foothills. Some stone images of the Sena school, which had acquired the ornate features of contemporary Kanarese sculpture, were brought to Nepal by Nānyadeva and his successors. Again, during the twelfth century, the Muslim conquest of Bengal led to an exodus of refugee artists to Nepal from there. It was then that the Eastem Indian tradition was subtly reinterpreted in Nepal.

Under the early Mallas (1200-1481), Nepali art, architecture and sculpture reached its climax in the thirteenth century and A-ni-ko carried the art of Nepal to Tibet and China. The image of the sun-god below the Thapahiti Fountain at Patan and the image of Garuḍa in front of the 'five roofed' or Nyātapola temple at Bhadgaun may be mentioned as examples of Nepal's stone sculpture in the 11th and 12th centuries respectively. The stone image of Gaurī at Devapatan, which belongs to the early thirteenth century, is also especially noteworthy. According to an inscription on its pedestal, this image of Gaurī emerging out of the lotus was erected to commemorate the death of a full-grown girl. Apart from its artistic qualities, it is one of the few early images that mention the name of the sculptor, one Nandapāla.

There is an image of the sun-god at Banepa, dated A.D. 1393. It belongs to the period of the feudatory chief Madanarāma Varddhana (1382-1395) and is another example of the very few Nepali works of art which mention the name of the artist themselves. The sculptors of this image mentioned were Rājamūlamī and Jayatamūlamī. The Banepa image of the sun-god, with a lotus in full bloom in both hands, riding on a chariot drawn by seven horses is remarkable from the viewpoint of the evolution of Nepali sculpture and foreshadows the developments in this field to the end of the Malla period. The images of various gods and goddesses, and specially those of the *boddhisattva* Avalokiteśvara and those of Vishnu, sculpted during the medieval period, are heavy in their physical build and are characterized by rotundity. The design of the image and of the setting and ornaments has also become more ornate and florid compared to those of the earlier period which are simpler in concept. However, the above-mentioned image of the sun-god may be cited as a remarkable example of medieval stone sculpture which from this time on seems to suffer a gradual decline.

By the sixteenth century, the Mallas had established themselves in power in the three Kingdoms of the Kathmandu Valley. It was during the last phase of Newari creative art that a myriad of anthropomorphic representations of tantric concepts used in contemplative exercises (*sadhanā*) found expression in images of frenzied grandeur.

As a matter of fact after the tenth century, stone-sculptures in Nepal were inferior to the bronzes, while metal images, both cast and repousse, retained their quality until the end of the sixteenth century, and, in some cases, carried it on into the nineteenth century. The only stone sculpture which deserves mention after the 10th century is the image of Surya (1065) at Thapathiti in Patan. The finest creative artists of the later period were workers in metal and wood. The different phases of the woodcarver's art have not as yet been categorized nor have those of the workers in rock crystal, ivory, human bones, and dry lacquer.

The fourteenth and the fifteenth centuries abounded in new creations typical of the evolving style of metal work. With an unbounded zeal, the tantric images were cast from the mid-fifteenth to the eighteenth centuty. The principle of the *unio mystica* finds expression in the sexual embrace of male and female figures. The male figure symbolises the active compassion (*karuṇā*) or the means or method (*upāya*) and the female figure represents supreme quiescent wisdom or gnosis (*prajñā*), or the void (*śūnyatā*), the symol of the absolute. Buddha, in his human form, penetrates *prajñā* and seeks confirmation of his Buddhahood. The male is the means and the female is the end, and together they symbolize the realization of the absolute. The fierce form of Buddha, Heruka in union with his partner, the Adamantine-Sow (*Vajravarāhī*) is called Hevajra. The twelve armed, four-headed deity with his normal-handed *Prajñā* clasping his waist in passionate sexual embrace is the Herukacakra Samvara of Nepal, the Yidam Sang-dui of Tibet. While dancing in union with his partner, this fierce human manifestation of Buddha tramples on the Hindu gods Brahma, Indra, Vishnu and Shiva as *māras* (evil ones).

The *sādhana*, or injunction for contemplation, and the making of these images, had originated in India centuries earlier as part of the rituals connected with the practice of the Vajra and Sahaja cult. Dr. Stella Kramrisch has pointed out that

> in the fifteenth to the eighteenth century in Nepal, those ancient symbols became quickened not with new meaning but with new life, and the ability arose to project into the sanctioned forms an emotional immediacy amounting to frenzy, whether in the experience of the tremendous or the horrendous.[4]

There was a time when the Nepali school of metal statuary was regarded merely as a sub-branch of the Tibetan school with which the western scholars and critics had become familiar at an earlier date. Sometimes the Nepali and Tibetan schools were even grouped together as the Tibeto-Nepalese school. However, there is no such confusion now and the prevailing opinion is that Nepal, rather than Tibet, was the prime inspiration in the field. The following comments of Ananda Coomaraswamy, the editor of the Indian art magazine *Rupam* on this point are highly appropriate:

> We have more than once commented on the fact that out and out Nepalese images are labelled and described in many museums as Tibetan works, and the whole relation of Tibetan art to Nepalese art has been misunderstood or deliberately ignored. The Lamaistic

> school was the result of a direct pupilage to the Nepalese tutors; and although it developed many special features, the groundwork of the Nepalese style was always a staple part of the Tibetan work. Evidences are now pointing to the fact that many Nepalese images must have been made to order for the use of Tibetan worshippers.[5]

Nepali brassware i.e., incense burners, candelabras, vases, and religious and secular vessels of other types are admired both for their practical utility and their high aesthetic quality. Newari artisans have attained a high level of excellence in the field of metal statuary. In this sphere, they have exercised a remarkable influence on the art of the whole Indian subcontinent. Commenting on the importance of the Nepali school in the history of Indian art, one authority states that the former continued the best tradition of Indian sculpture at a time when Indian art, in India itself, was in a state of decline. Another writer comments that the better specimens of Nepali metal statuary of the seventeenth and eighteenth centuries have proven to be the most representative and exceptional masterpieces of Indian art.

Although early Nepali metal statuary also possessed considerable aesthetic quality, it was only during the period between the sixteenth and the eighteenth centuries that this form of artistic expression reached its zenith in Nepal. Ananda Coomaraswamy has succinctly summed up the history of the evolution of Nepali metal image-casting in the following words:

> On the whole, we may say that Nepalese art has remained throughout decidely more conservative than that of the plains, a natural consequence of isolation. In the older Nepalese figures, the Indian character is altogether predominant, and there is no suggestion whatever of anything Mongolian; they recall the work of the Gupta period and are, perhaps, as near as we can hope to get to examples of Taranath's 'school of the east' and they cannot be wholly unrelated to works of the Bengali school of Dhiman and Bitapala. They are characterized by a very full modelling of the flesh and almost florid features; the bridge of the nose is markedly rounded and the lips full. On the other hand, those of a later date, and up to modern times, are no longer so robust and fleshy, but svelte and slender-waisted and more sharply contoured: the nose becomes aquiline, some times even hooked, the lips clearcut and thin, thus the development involves an attenuation and refinement of the forms: at the

same time iconographically, the forms are often much more complicated and the ornament richer.[6]

Painting

A wide range of religious and social considerations seems to have inspired Nepali paintings. Pictures were painted to celebrate the occasion of the attainment of a ripe old age of seventy-seven years (*uṣṇiṣa-vijayotsava*); to comfort the souls that had already departed to heaven; to commemorate participation in ceremonies characterized by the performance of fasts and fire sacrifices; to visualize tantric concepts for meditative purposes (*sādhana*); to introduce books; to bring good luck to patrons and to popularize the religious stories of the Buddhist Jātaka Tales or Avadhāna Stories and the Hindu *Purāṇas.*

The earliest specimens of Nepali painting which have been discovered so far are illustrations on palmleaf manuscripts of the eleventh and the twelfth centuries and the pictures on the wooden book covers that date back to the tenth century. There is a thousand-year-old picture on the wooden covers of a book called *Prajñāpāramitā* that dates from about A.D. 920. The pictures of the five Buddhas and four Saviouresses are drawn on the top wooden cover. On the bottom cover are pictures of tantric deities such as *Prajñāpāramitā* (Perfection of Wisdom), Vajrasattva (Diamond-Being) and the divine ladies taking part in worship with flowers, conches, and lamps. A picture of Shiva-Pārvatī encircled by other gods and goddesses on the wooden covers of the book called *Niśvasa Tantra*, dated A.D.1060, is in keeping with the *śākta* tantric tradition. As an example of the Vaishnava tradition in painting we may cite wooden book covers depicting Vishnu holding in his four hands a conch, a wheel, a club, and a lotus. The representations are eleven in number and severally enclosed by arch gates (*toraṇa*). These pictures go back to the rule of Abhaya Malla in the thirteenth century. Pictures of Mañjuśrī and Mahāmañjuśrī, contained in a book called *Aṣṭasahaṣrikā-Prajñāpāramitā*, dating from the twelfth century, and pictures of five Buddhas and their Prajñās (female counterparts), five Saviouresses (*Tārās*) each of them beautifully painted on a separate page in a book of palmleaves, dating from the thirteenth century and preserved in the Bhaktapur picture gallery, are outstanding examples of this art form.

The above pictures are strongly influenced by the Pala form of Eastern Indian painting. All Nepali paintings, whether on palmleaf, paper, wood or cloth are in gouache, that is to say, they are painted in opaque colours which have been ground in water and mingled with a preparation of gum. The Nepali painter is not primarily interested in modelling by colour, shading and line, and even when he is interested in doing so, he is not too successful.

Gradually, the meticulous forms of miniature painting, with or without modelling, gave way to the more schematic, or to state the truth, rather sketchy, cursive outlines. This technique was suited to cope with the demand for paintings by the Gelugpa Sect which was founded in Tibet by Tsong Kapa (c. 1357-1409). Nepali artists were sent for to paint in the Nor monastery in southern Tibet, and the influence of A-ni- ko and his party of eighty Nepali artists still seemed to prevail there. Hierarchs of the Sakya school were painted by them on cloth. Those Nepali artists had several religious paintings to their credit.

Apart from miniature painting one finds larger paintings known as *pauva* or *paubāhā* in Newari. Two styles of painting were in evidence in Nepal at the time, both of them rather schematic or ordered forms of painting: the maṇḍala and the *paṭā*. *Paṭā* (Sk.)is a general term for a 'banner painting', but is often used in contradistinction to a *maṇḍala* painting. A *maṇḍala* is a diagram of a *sādhana* and the entire circle of deities to be visualised in the course of the yogic meditation. It is designed to chart one's way out of the chaos of the subconscious and the complicated problems of the world. The painting of a *maṇḍala* demands a great deal of accuracy and precision from the painter and is not suited to the needs of creative experience and freedom. A *patā* is a painting of a single deity or a small group of deities selected from the *maṇḍala*. In this case there is more scope for the urge of creative experience and hence the *patā* tends to be less rigid.

Maṇḍalas painted in Nepal are less rigid in their organization than those painted in the Tibetan monasteries. In the case of the Nepali *maṇḍala*, the central square houses the main deity with greater freedom as in a *patā*, and the scenes around the encompassing circle of cemeteries are not always illustrated. Even when they are not illustrated, the earlier paintings are still full of narrative and leave no space for the images of the lesser divinities. Nepali paintings, whether *maṇḍala* or *patā*, are on coarse cloth whereas the Tibetan paintings are painted on fine cotton cloth.

In Nepal itself there are many such paintings preserved among the collections of tantric manuscripts kept in the secret tantric chapels (*āgā*) in *vihāras*, temples and private homes, but they cannot be seen by the general public. They depict Buddhist *maṇḍalas*, Hindu tantric *yantras* and a wide variety of secret tantric deities. Mention must be made of the painting of Bhairavānanda and Kubjikā, which belongs to the reign of Jyotira Malla around A.D.1418. It is not only remarkable from the artistic point of view but is also an accurate representation of tantric concepts and ritualistic forms and designs on a grand scale. Another notable feature of this painting is that the painter's name, Tejarāma, is given. Thus Tejarāma is one of the few masters of Nepali medieval painting whose name has come down to us. In most other works of art, the artist's name is not mentioned, and only the name of the patron or donor is given.

A fifteenth century (A.D.1401) painting of Herukacakra Saṃvara shows the sixteen-handed fierce (Heruka) aspect of Buddha Aksobya in passionate sexual embrace with his female counterpart (*prajñā*), the Adamantine Sow (*Vajravarāhī*), with the principal Hindu gods and goddesses of Shaivism lying prostrate at his feet as a mark of respect to him. This *patā* is treasured in the secret room (*āgā*) at Jana Baha, the Macchendranath shrine in Kathmandu.

The period between the latter half of the fourteenth century and the late sixteenth century was characterized by works of touching nobility and concentrated power both in painting and in sculpture. In this connection, mention must be made of the Nepali *patā* which is treasured in the Rijksmuseum voor Volkenkunde in Leiden, in the Netherlands. According to its inscription, it represents Amoghapāśa Lokeśvāra of the Mahabhuta temple at Bhadgaun, and its purpose is to bring prosperity and a large number of children to the donors. This painting is reproduced in Dr. Stella Kramrisch's *The Art of Nepal.*[7] The Malla rulers of Nepal patronized painting and there are many paintings that mention the Malla Kings as patrons. By the end of the sixteenth century, Nepali painting had begun to show the influence of Rajasthani as well as Chinese-Tibetan styles. Although the Nepali masters were the teachers of Tibetan artists in the fourteenth and the fifteenth centuries, the Tibetan style had begun to make its influence felt in Nepal by the middle of the seventeenth century. In the traditional Nepali style, occasionally found as late as the mid-eighteenth century, the images are set against a flat opaque background, but a Tibetan painting (*thangkha*) of that time presents its images as part of a transparent curtain against the background of a Chinese landscape fantasy. Traditional Nepali painting resisted the intrusion of this landscape background until the nineteenth century.

Another type of painting of this period is the narrative scroll. Narrative scrolls were long known in India, and, when transferred to the wall, they had provided long friezes in the Ajanta caves as early as the beginning of the Christian era. In Nepal these scrolls acquired a sense of spatial allusion about this time but from a different source. It came through the Rajasthani style of painting from India. Rajasthani painting, under the impact of Muslim and particularly Mogul painting, acquired some features and perspectives of both Persian and Western Renaissance painting. Painters of Nepali narrative scrolls found it difficult to resist the temptation of imitating features of the Rajasthani style once they were exposed to it. There is in the British Museum a long Nepali narrative scroll (dated: A.D.1705) which illustrates the story of Buddha's life. It displays not only the kind of western perspective which was introduced into Nepal by seventeenth century Rajasthani painting but also includes Indian figures both in Hindu and Muslim costume.

The wall paintings in the Bhadgaun palace are done in this new style. Murals or frescoes can still be seen on the walls of the buildings in the main quadrangles of the Bhadgaun palace such as the Kumarīcok and Mūlcok. They date back to the reign of Jitāmitra Malla toward the end of the seventeenth century and the time immediately following his reign in the eighteenth century. The seventeenth century frescoes on the walls of the ground floor are of a higher quality than the murals on the walls of the second floor which reveal the decadent features of eighteenth century Nepali painting.

NOTES

1. Percy Brown, *Picturesque Nepal*, London, Adam and Charles Black, 1912, pp. 152-53.
2. Ulrich Wiesner, *Nepalese Temple Architecture, Its Characteristics and Its Relations to Indian Development*, Leiden, E.J. Brill, 1978, pp. 106-9.
3. E. Alexander Powell, *The Last Home of Mystery*, New York, Garden City Publishing Co., 1929, pp. 216-17; pp. 218-19.
4. Stella Kramrisch, *The Art of Nepal*, Philadelphia Asia House Gallery, 1964, p. 146.
5. Ananda Coomaraswamy, 'A Tibeto-Nepalese Image of Maitreya,' *Rupam*, No. 11 (July, 1922), p. 73.
6. Ananda Coomaraswamy, 'A Nepalese Tara,' *Rupam*, No. 6 (April 1921), p. 1.
7. Stella Kramrisch, p. 146.

Chronology of The Rulers of The Nepal Valley (Khaldo) (currently known as the Kathmandu Valley)

Table I. The Rulers of the Licchavi Period, C. A.D. 400-879.

Rulers	A.D. Conversions of Verified Dates from Saka and Mānadeva Era Inscriptions
Vṛṣadeva	C. A.D. 400
Śaṅkaradeva	C. A.D. 425
Dharmadeva	C. A.D. 450
Mānadeva	C. A.D. 464-505
Mahīdeva	a few months
Vasantadeva	A.D. 506-532
Manudeva	
Vāmanadeva	A.D. 538
Rāmadeva	A.D. 545
Gaṇadeva	A.D. 557-565
Gaṅgadeva	A.D. 567
Mānadeva II (founder of the Manadeva era beginning A.D. 576)	A.D. 576
Śivadeva I	A.D. 590-604
Amusvarman	A.D. 605-621
Udayadeva	A.D. 621
Dhruvadeva + Jiṣṇu Gupta	A.D. 624-625
Bhimārjunadeva + Jiṣṇu Gupta	A.D. 631-633
Bhimārjunadeva + Viṣṇu Gupta	A.D. 640-641
Narendradeva	A.D. 643-649
Śivadeva II	A.D. 685-701
Jayadeva II	A.D. 713-733
Śivadeva III	A.D. 750
Manadeva III	A.D. 756
Gaṇadeva II	
Balirāja	A.D. 826
Bāladeva	A.D. 847
Mānadeva IV	A.D. 875

Table II. Rulers of the Early Medieval Period, C.A.D. 879-1200

Rulers and Probable Rulers	Reign or Approximate Reign in A.D.
Rāghavadeva	879
Saṅkaradeva I	920
/Sahadeva/	
/Vikramadeva/	
Gunakamadeva I	980-990
Narendradeva I + Udayadeva	998
Udayadeva	1004
Nirbhayadeva	1005
Nirbhayadeva + Rudradeva I	1008
Bhojadeva	1011
Rudradeva I + Bhojadeva	1012
Bhojadeva + Rudradeva I + Lakshmikamadeva I	1015
Lakṣhmīkāmadeva I	1041
(Jayakāmadeva)	
Bhāskaradeva	1039-1048
Baladeva + Yisadeva	1048-1060
Pradyumanakāmadeva	1060-1066
Nāgārjunadeva	1066-1069
Sankaradeva II	1069-1082
Vāmadeva	1082-1085
Harṣadeva	1085-1098
Śivadeva = Siṃhadeva	1098-1126
Indradeva	1126-1136
Mānadeva	1136-1140
Narendradeva II	1140-1147
Ānandadeva	1147-1167
Rudradeva II	1167-1175
Amṛtadeva	1176-1178
Someśvaradeva	1178-1183/85
Guṇakāmadeva II	1184-1187
Lakṣhmīkāmadeva II	1192-1197
Vijayakāmadeva	1192-1200

Table III. The Rulers of the Early Malla Period, A.D. 1200-1482

Rulers	Regnal Dates in A.D.
Arti Malla	1200-1216
Abhaya Malla	1216-1255
Jayadeva	1255-1258
Jayabhīmadeva	1258-1271
Jayaśiha Malla	1271-1274
Ananta Malla	1274-1308
Jayānandadeva	1308-1320
Jayari Malla	1320-1344
Jayarājadeva	1347-1361
Jayārjunadeva	1361-1382
Jayasthitirāja Malla	1382-1395
Jayadharma Malla	1395-1408
Jayajyotir Malla	1408-1428
Yakṣha Malla	1428-1482

Table IV. The Rulers of the Independent Kingdom of Kathmandu, A.D. 1482-1768

Malla Dynasty	Approximate regnal years in A.D.
Ratna	1482-1520
Sūrya	1520-1529
Amara = Narendra	1529-1560
Mahendra	1560-1574
Sadaśiva	1574-1578
Śivasiṃha	1578-1617
Lakṣhmīnarasiṃha	1617-1641
Pratāpa	1641-1674
Nṛpendra	1674-1680
Pārthivendra	1680-1687
Bhūpālendra	1687-1700
Bhāskara = Mahendrasiṃha	1700-1722
Jagajjaya	1722-1733
Jayaprakāśa	1734-1768
(but interrupted by the reign of an infant son, Jyotiprakāśa (1746-1752)	

Table V. The Rulers of the Independent Kingdom of Patan, A.D. 1482-1768

Malla dynasty, mahāpātras, and one shah king	Approximate regnal years in A.D.
Rāya Malla, his brothers and a nephew in varying combinations	1482-1536
Viṣṇusiṃha, the pradhana mahāpātra and ruling	1536
Patan independently of the Mallas	1546-1556
Purandarasiṃha, alone or with his brothers	1556-1596
Malla rule established by	
(Śivasiṃha Malla between 1596 and 1599)	1617
Siddhinarasiṃha	1618-1661
Śrīnivāsa	1661-1685
Yoganarendra	1685-1705
Lokaprakāśa	1705-1706
(Yoganarendra's daughter Yogamati's infant son)	
Indra Malla	1706-1709
(Yoganarendra's eldest sister Manimati's son)	
Mahindra Malla=	1709-1715
Viranarasiṃha	1709
(a rival who had a brief rule)	
Ṛddhinarasimha	1715-1717
Bhāskara=Mahendrasiṃha	1717-1722
Yogaprakāśa Malla	1722-1729
Viṣṇu Malla	1729-1745
Rajyaprakāśa Malla	1745-1758
Viśvajit	1758-1760
Jayaprakāśa Malla of Kathmandu	1761
Ranajit Malla of Kathmandu	1762-1763
Jayaprakāśa Malla of Bhagdaun	1763
Dalamardana Śaha	1764-1765
Tejanarasiṃha Malla	1765-1768

Table VI. The Rulers of the Independent Kingdom of Bhadgaun, A.D. 1482-1769

Malla Dynasty	Approximate regnal years in A.D.
Rāya and others	1482-1495
Rāya alone	1496-1505
Bhuvana	1505-1518
Jita+Prāna (Prāna ruling alone after 1534)	1518-1545
Viśva	1545-1559
Trailokya	1559-1614
Jagajjyotir	1614-1637
Nareśa	1637-1643
Jagatprakāśa	1643-1672
Jitamitra	1672-1696
Bhupatīndra	1696-1722
Ranajita	1722-1769

BIBLIOGRAPHY

Bharati, Agehananda. *The Tantric Tradition.* London: Rider, 1965.

Bhattacharya, Benoytosh. *An Introductin to Buddhist Esoterism.* Second Revised ed. Chowkhamba Sanskrit Series, Vol. 36. Varanasi: Chowkhamba, 1964.

Brown, Percy. *Picturesque Nepal.* London: Adam and Charles Black, 1912.

Coomaraswami, Ananda Kumar. 'A Nepalese Tara,' *Rupam*, No. 6 (April 1921).

——————'A Tibeto--Nepalese Image of Maitreya,' *Rupam*, No. 11 (July 1922).

Cunningham, A. *Ancient Geography of India* . Ed. S.N. Majumdar Sastri. Calcutta, 1924.

Fleet, John Faithfull. *Corpus Inscriptionum Indicarum.* Vol. 2, 3rd Revised Edition. *Inscriptions of the Early Gupta Kings and Their Successors* . Varanasi, Indological Book House, 1970.

Giuseppe, Father. 'Account of the Kingdom of Nepal, 1768-71,' *Asiatick Researches* 2 (1901).

Gnoli, Raniero. *Nepalese Inscriptions in Gupta Characters.* Serie Orientale Roma X. Materials for the Study of Nepalese History and Culture No. 2. Rome: Istituto Itialiano per il Medio ed Estremo Orientale.

Gosh, N.N. *Early History of India.* Allahabad, 1935.

Gurung, Harka Bahadur. 'Geographic Setting', in *Nepal, A Profile.* Kathmandu: Nepal Council of Applied Economic Research, 1970.

Indraji, Bhagavanlal. 'Twenty-three Inscriptions from Nepal with some Considerations on the Chronology of Nepal,' Translated from Gujurati by G. Buhler, *Indian Antiquary*, Vol IX (1880).

Khanal, Mohan Prasad. 'Itihās Saṃsodhanko Kehī Saṃsodhan,' *Ancient Nepal* 3 (October, 1970).

——————'Rājā Bhaškara Malla (Mahindra Siṃha) kā Viśayamā Saṃsodhan ra Nirṇaya,' *Ancient Nepal* 9 (October, 1969).

Kirkpatrick, Colonel. *An Account of the Kingdom of Nepaul*, being the Substance of Observations Made during a Mission to that Country in the Year 1793. 1811. Reprint: Bibliotheca Himalayica, Series I, Vol. 3. New Delhi: Manjusri Publishing House, 1969.

Kolver, Bernhard and Hemraj Sakya. *Documents from the Rudravarna - Mahavihara, Patan.* Sankt Augustin: VGH-Wissenschaft-sveralag, 1985.

Kramrisch, Stella. *The Art of Nepal.* Philadelphia: Asia House Gallery, 1964.

Lamsal, Deviprasad, ed. *Bhāṣā Vaṃśāvalī* Part II. Puratatva Prakāśan Mālā 38. Kathmandu: National Library, 2023 Vikram Sambat.

Landon, Percival. *Nepal.* London: Constable and Co. 1928.

Levi, Sylvain. *Le Nepal.* Three Volumes. Annals de Musee Guimet, Bibliotheque d'Etudes, Vols. 17, 18, 19. Paris: Ernest Leroux, 1905.

Majumdar, R.C. 'The Eras of Nepal,' in *Journal of the Asiatic Society* (1959) I:1, 47-49.

Malla, Kamal P. 'Nepālavaṃśāvalī: A Complete Version of the Kaisher Vamsavali,' *Contributions to Nepalese Studies* XII, 2 (April 1985).

Pant, Mahesh and Dinesh Raj. 'Nepālkhālḍomā Pālpālī Rājā Mukunda Senko Hamalā,' *Pūrṇimā* 45:7.

Paudel, Nayanath. *Bhāṣā Vaṃśāvalī* Part One. Puratatva Prakāśan Mālā 21. Kathmandu, Nepal National Library, 2020 Vikram Sambat.

Petech, Luciano. *Mediaeval History of Nepal* (c. 750-1482). Second, Thoroughly Revised Edition. Serie Orientale Roma LIV. Rome: Instituto Italiano per il Medio ed Estremo Oriente, 1984.

Powell, E. Alexander. *The Last Home of Mystery.* New York: Garden City Publishing Co., 1929.

Rajvamsi, Shankar Man. 'Mahindrasiṃha (Bhāskara Malla) ko Tāmrapatra ra Thyasko Aitihāsik Vyākhyā,' *Pūrṇimā* 11: 55-60.

———'Siddhinarasiṃha Mallabhanda Agāḍikā Pāṭankā Śāsakharūkā Kehī Tāḍspatra,' *Pūrṇimā* 12:17-22.

———'Yoganarendra Mallakā Uttarādhikarī,' *Pūrnimā* 6:37-44.

Regmi, Dilli Raman. *Ancient Nepal.* First Edition. Calcutta: Firma K. L. Mukhopadhyay, 1960.

————*Inscriptions of Ancient Nepal*. Three Volumes. New Delhi: Abhinav Publications, 1983.

————*Medieval Nepal*. Four Volumes. Calcutta: Firma K.L. Mukhopadhyay, 1965-66.

Regmi, Jagadish Candra. *Prācīn Nepālko Rajnītik Itihās*. Kathmandu: Royal Nepal Academy, 2035 Vikram Sambat.

Sakya, Hemraj. *Śivadeva Saṃskārita Uṅkule Śrī Rudravarṇa Mahāvihāra Sthita Tālpatra-Abhilekh*. Patan: Buddha Jayanti Samiti, 2524 Buddha Samvat.

Sakya, Hemraj and T.R. Vaidya. eds. *Medieval Nepal*. Colophons and Inscriptions. Kathmandu, Vaidya, 1970.

Sharma, Prayag Raj. 'The Land System of the Licchavis in Nepal,' *Kailash* (1983) X, 1-2:11-62.

Shastri, Hara Prasad. *A Catalogue of Palm Leaf and Selected Paper Manuscripts Belonging to the Darbar Library, Nepal*. Two Volumes. Calcutta: Baptist Mission Press, 1915.

Slusser, Mary S. *Nepal Mandala*, A Cultural Study of the Kathmandu Valley. Two Volumes. Princeton: Princeton University Press, 1982.

Tucci, Giuseppe. Nepal, *The Discovery of the Malla*. Translated from the Italian by Lovett Edwards. New York: E. P. Dutton, 1962.

————*Preliminary Report on Two Scientific Expeditions in Nepal*. Serie Orientale Roma X. Rome: Istituto Italiano per il Media Estremo Orientale, 1956.

Vajracarya, Dhanavajra. 'Cautārā Bhagirata Bhaiyā,' *Pūrṇimā* 5:21-31.

————*Licchavīkālkā Abhilekh*. Institute of Nepal and Asian Studies, Historical Collections Series, No. 6. Kathmandu: INAS, 1973.

————'Madhyakālik Nepālkā ek Prakhyāt Rājā Śivadeva,' *Contributions to Nepalese Studies*, 8,1 (1980).

————'Śaktiśālī Bhārdār Rāmavarddhanaharū ra Tatkālik Nepāl,' *Pūrṇimā* 7:12-36.

————'Yoganarendra Mallako Rājyābhisek,' *Pūrṇimā* 9:17-21.

Vajracarya, Dhanavajra and Kamal P. Malla eds, tr. The *Gopālarāja-vaṃśāvalī*. Nepal Research Centre Publications No. 9. Wiesbaden: Franz Steiner Verlag, 1985.

Vajracarya, Dhanavajra and Tek Bahadur Shrestha. *Dolakhāko Aitihāsik Rūprekhā*. Institute of Nepal and Asian Studies, Historical Collections Series 8. Kathmandu: INAS, 2031 Vikram Sambat.

——————*Nuvakoṭko Aitihāsik Rūprekhā*. Kathmandu: INAS, 2032 Vikram Sambat.

Walsh, E.H., 'The Coinage of Nepal', *Journal of the Royal Asiatic Society of Great Britain and Ireland* (July 1908).

Wiesner, Ulrich. *Nepalese Temple Architecture*, Its Characteristics and its Relations to Indian Development. Studies in South Asian Culture edited for the Institute of South Asian Archaeology, University of Amsterdam by J.E. Van Lohuizen-de Leeuw. Volume VIII. Leiden: E.J. Brill, 1978.

Wright, Daniel, ed. *History of Nepal*, Translated from the Parbatiya by Munshi Shew Shunker Sing and Pandit Sri Guruanand, with an introductory sketch of the country and people of Nepal by the editor. Calcutta: Ranjan Gupta, 1877.

INDEX